THE LAST MI Moore

The last men's book you'll ever need

Dave Moore has a
curiosity.

The Late William F. Buckley
Best-selling author and TV personality

Dave's ability to prompt and encourage a thoughtful approach
to one's life is a unique gift. His teaching has been the recent
catalyst for my own desire to grow in all areas of life.

Cody Carlson
Former NFL quarterback

This is an unusual attempt to bring men to a conservative
Christian understanding of self, family, and world through
a very contemporary sense of humor. Moore, founder and
president of Two Cities Ministries, recognizes the perils
of sexual temptation, materialism, work, and what he calls
"the shrinking American soul," and his first line of defense is
"the simplicity and purity of devotion to Christ." His book
should have a strong appeal to men floundering for a Christian
grasp of the world or Christian men struggling to be good
husbands and fathers.

Library Journal

How do you get modern (and postmodern) men to go deep in their faith, their relationships, and their thoughts? That's the $64,000 question that David Moore seems to have discovered the answer to in *The Last Men's Book You'll Ever Need*. Read it from cover to cover. Read it in snatches. Read it in bits and pieces. Read it in groups. Read it alone. Just be sure to read it.

George Grant
Best-selling author and pastor of Parish Presbyterian Church

This is a "get to the point" book. Actually, it is not SO manly that a woman wouldn't benefit from reading it. I (being a woman) actually didn't skip any chapter (or page, for that matter). The book was worth my time; I looked forward to each chapter. In addition, I look forward to reading many of the titles mentioned in the notes at the end of each chapter. This book could actually serve as a resource for delving into other books (current and classics). For that reason, the book appeals to the casual reader as well as readers who desire a deeper look.

Regina Love
Posted on Amazon.com

Dave Moore has a new book that looks quite good . . . it is serious Puritan-esque theology told in a non-Puritan way.

Justin Taylor
Between Two Worlds Blog

THE LAST MEN'S BOOK YOU'LL EVER NEED

THE LAST MEN'S BOOK YOU'LL EVER NEED

WHAT THE BIBLE SAYS ABOUT GUY STUFF

DAVID MOORE

B&H
PUBLISHING GROUP
Nashville, Tennessee

978-0-8054-4681-4

Published by B&H Publishing Group,
Nashville, Tennessee

Dewey Decimal Classification: 248.842
Subject Heading: MEN \ CHRISTIAN LIFE

2 3 4 5 6 7 8   11 10 09 08

Dedication

The writing of a book is never isolated from the realities of living "east of Eden." I had two graphic reminders of this in 2007.

Rich Gabel demonstrated in his suffering and death what it truly means to be a man. His quiet, steady confidence in the goodness of God was a marvel to behold. I am grateful for experiencing much of it up close. My sister-in-law, Linda, and her two children, Jonathan and Lauren, were blessed to know such a man.

Tony and Karen Debenport lost their dear daughter Elesha to cancer. Tony's eulogy was a profound tribute to the grace of God. Tony's honesty with the pain of terrible loss makes his faithfulness to God all that more compelling. He models one of his favorite verses:

> But it is still my consolation,
> And I rejoice in unsparing pain,
> That I have not denied the
> words of the Holy One. (Job 6:10)

Contents

Acknowledgments

I called on a number of friends to offer input on this writing project. They offered much encouragement, insight, and lovingly prodded me to be clear. Authors are accustomed to saying that whatever failings remain are their responsibility alone. It is a wise thing to mention, so I am glad to admit that the buck, or in this case, the book, stops with me.

Several of these guys go back to my college days. They have the goods on me. Hopefully, that made their input more valuable. I am indebted to David Drell, Tod Barrett, David Storm, Steve Carr, Blake Mosher,

Roger Berry, Danny Smith, Dennis Ryan, Bill Ferrell, John Steele, David Lill, Mark Cotnam, Tony Debenport, Darin Maurer, Doug Ruby, Ben Burns, Colby Kinser, John Freeman, David Smith, John Lierman, Joel Altsman, Jim McBride, Steve Crone, Kurt Richardson, David Backus, Vaughn Brock, Tim Taylor, Brooke Butler, Ryan McDonald, Nolan Egbert, Wayne Hammond, Warren Culwell, Steve Kwan, David Lill, Andrew Lawson, Roger Medd, Cody Carlson, Tom Wright, Bob Pyne, and Gil Hooper.

Professor John Lierman deserves special mention. John took much time out of his busy schedule to provide extremely detailed critiques of each chapter. John's critiques could be a bit daunting (lots of red ink!), but they definitely pushed me to do better work.

At Two Cities Ministries, I am greatly helped by an omnicompetent assistant in Barb Miaso. Blake Freeburg gives amazing technological assistance. Our board (Roger Berry, Gil Hooper, David Lill, and Tim Taylor) provides sage counsel and wonderful encouragement.

Len Goss, formerly at B&H Publishing Group, was terrific to work with. Len is well-respected nationally for good reasons. I was blessed to have him on my side. Len graciously handled a myriad of questions and concerns with characteristic aplomb. I am grateful to Kim Stanford of B&H for her quick replies to my other questions. Yes, I have lots of questions.

My own "triumvirate of grace" inspires, encourages, and makes me want to do my best: my faithful wife, Doreen, and our two sons, David and Christopher.

Introduction

Men are odd creatures. That's not to say women aren't, but this is a book for men. Women should feel free to read it. In fact, most of this book easily applies to either sex. I, being of the masculine type, write with men in view. At the very least, women ought to read this book to have more awareness of the sorry excuses we men sometimes give.

The title for this book is obviously tongue-in-cheek. I do write with the hope that this book offers enough wisdom to slow down the sales of faddish men's books. As a result, if men begin to redirect their book buying money to more worthy materials, I will be an extremely satisfied writer.

This book is divided into six sections. Not seven, mind you, but six. I would like to start a revolution of six. I know seven is the perfect number and many authors like to use it, but I would like to start a trend with the number six. Granted, it is part of the "mark of the beast," but then again this is a book for men.

All the chapter titles could easily fit under the first part: "Your Relationship with God." In that sense the placing of the respective chapters under the various sections is somewhat arbitrary. However, I have sought to place the chapters where they seemed most relevant for the logic and flow of the book.

The Last Men's Book You'll Ever Need is obviously a quick read. Space limitations forced me to spend significant time thinking through how best to structure the book. It actually was a fun process. The brevity of the various chapters means that issues can't be developed in great detail. I do try to approach these issues in a way that provides an angle that many of the other "men's" books don't. Please feel free to pick and choose what chapters you want to read first.

You will find discussion and application questions at the end of each chapter. These questions are designed to spawn further conversation and, ultimately, foster the desire to grow spiritually. They are well suited for both small group study and personal reflection.

I wrote this book from the conviction that a touch of humor and a thoroughly biblical message can teach us "old truths in fresh ways." There are potential pitfalls with this approach, but I have decided that the advantages outweigh the risks. But make no mistake about it: This is a serious book that hopefully will give a few good laughs along the way. G. K. Chesterton's words are worth considering: "For solemnity flows out of men naturally; but laughter is a leap. It is easy to be heavy: hard to be light. Satan fell by the force of gravity." Charles Spurgeon, a nineteenth-century preacher who took God very seriously, had a deep appreciation for humor:

> I must confess that I would rather hear people laugh than I would see them asleep in the

house of God; and I would rather get the truth into them through the medium of ridicule than I would have the truth neglected, or leave the people to perish through lack of reception of the truth. I do believe in my heart that there may be as much holiness in a laugh as in a cry; and that, sometimes, to laugh is the better thing of the two, for I may weep, and be murmuring, and repining [expressing discontent], and thinking all sorts of bitter thoughts against God; while, at another time, I may laugh the laugh of sarcasm against sin. . . . I do not know why ridicule is to be given up to Satan as a weapon to be used against us, and not to be employed by us as a weapon against him.

Martin Luther and others agree with that assessment.

Speaking of humor, I had the privilege during the summer of 2000 to interview the well-known political commentator, William F. Buckley, for a television special that aired nationally on PBS. You will read more about that in the book. In that wide-ranging interview,

Buckley told me that humor was "salubrious." I nodded knowingly, but later found out this means "that which promotes health." Indeed. Humor heals. Humor can be both relevant and life-giving.

Crude and bawdy humor is not difficult to come up with. Any observant person with a little bit of creativity can pull that off. However, I am persuaded that belief in God can stir us to have the best humor possible. God allows us to experience the difficulties of life, but put them in a bigger context. *There is another world* where every "tear will be wiped away" and joy will be without end.

Whatever your view of humor, there is no doubt that God is the most "salubrious" being in the universe. I pray this book makes you more convinced of that.

Notes

G. K. Chesterton's words are worth considering, G. K. Chesterton, *Orthodoxy: The Romance of Faith* (New York, NY: Doubleday, 1990), 121.

Charles Spurgeon, a nineteenth century preacher . . . C. H. Spurgeon, *Lectures to My Students* (Grand Rapids, MI: Zondervan Publishing Company, 1954), 389.

Martin Luther and others agree with that assessment. Luther's nemesis, Erasmus, said that many writers throughout history utilized humor effectively. *The Essential Erasmus*, trans. by John P. Dolan (New York, NY: Signet Classics, 1964), 99. The *Praise of Folly* is Erasmus's best-known book. One of my favorite parts is where Erasmus says, "Ignorance is bliss," and then goes on to explain how that works!

PART
ONE

Your Relationship
with God

Chapter 1

Stop the PowerPoint Presentations of the Christian Life!

You are supposed to behave in discussion groups at church. You know what I am talking about. There's an unwritten code of conduct. There are certain clear yet unstated expectations that all are supposed to abide by. Don't go off the Christian reservation with comments that might show some disagreement with the leader's lesson. Let me tell you about one of the times (yes, there have been others for yours truly!) when I cast the proverbial code of conduct to the wind.

About one hundred of us were sitting dutifully at our respective tables. The Sunday school leader, in this case a pastor, had just gone through teaching on his understanding of Christian growth. Along with his lesson, he provided a nice little chart that sought to show the pattern of growth that all Christians supposedly go through. The line that he plotted for the typical Christian did have some twists and turns on it. Here he was trying to show that our growth is not without struggle, a crucial thing to remember. However, his graph showed the line *always proceeding forward* in one direction. It eventually arrived at heaven. Granted, all Christians eventually arrive safely in heaven, but does the path always progress forward?

Our discussion group leader conscientiously followed his assigned duties. He wanted to know how the rest of us would apply the pastor's chart. The assumption was that the chart accurately reflected the Bible's teaching on Christian growth. I figured I'd better speak up right away. Here is what I said: "I can't apply the chart because I don't think it completely reflects what the Bible teaches about Christian growth." An awkward silence fell over our group. My wife who is somewhat used to my "m.o." in these situations didn't flinch. In fact, the simplistic rendering of the Christian life also bothered her. My wife is a very discerning woman!

Let's look briefly at why graphs and PowerPoint presentations of the Christian life rarely do justice in reflecting what the Scriptures teach.

Consider the many examples we see in the New Testament. We find a wide variety of people with different gifts, personalities, and struggles. Peter was different than Paul, and Paul was certainly different than Timothy. Just think about a few of these:

- Paul had a dramatic conversion and was courageous with the gospel, yet struggled with severe discouragement (see 2 Cor. 1:8–11; 7:5–6).
- Timothy didn't have a dramatic conversion, was a faithful pastor, but struggled with timidity (see 2 Tim. 1:1–7).

- Mary Magdalene, who once was demon-possessed, also had a dramatic conversion, but she did not deny Christ like Peter. And don't forget that Peter denied Christ three times. The graph of his spiritual life would show his line going backwards for a period of time.
- The Lord Himself picked Thomas, yet he struggled with doubts.

Many more examples could easily be added.

As Americans, we love a one-size-fits-all approach to Christian growth. Sameness is the American way. Sadly, too many American Christians do not appreciate that fellow believers have different gifts embodied in different personalities.

Acknowledging and appreciating the diversity of Christians presents a big problem for many churches: it undermines *efficiency*. Think about how influential the business model is on the American church. Language such as "we want everyone on the same page" is commonly used instead of the biblical idea of having unity amidst diverse gifts. Biblical unity *includes* diverse people anchored to the same truth struggling to love one another.

Diverse patterns of spiritual growth also appear outside the New Testament. One of my favorite examples is found in one my favorite books, *The Pilgrim's Progress*. John Bunyan knew human nature and did a great job of showing that different people struggle with different things. One of Bunyan's characters, Mr. Fearing, was not tempted by worldly pleasures. Other believers in *The Pilgrim's Progress* were enticed by the "vanities" of the world, but not Mr. Fearing. As you might surmise from his name, Mr. Fearing struggled with fear. At one point in his pilgrimage to the Celestial City (heaven), he faced a rather treacherous stretch. Mr. Fearing was overcome with terror. Bunyan described the scene this way:

> But when he came to the entrance of the
> Valley of the Shadow of Death I thought
> I should have lost my man, not that he had any
> inclination to go back, that he always abhorred,
> but he was ready to die for fear. "O, the hob-
> goblins [demonic creatures] will have me, the

hobgoblins will have me," cried he, and I could not get him to stop.

So Mr. Fearing was not at all enticed by the various seductions of the world, but he was filled with dread when he considered whether he would safely make it to the Celestial City. Since Bunyan understood human nature and the grace of God much better than most, he was able then to pen these touching and, more importantly, true words:

> But this I took very great notice of, that this valley was as quiet while Mr. Fearing went through it as ever I knew it before or since. I suppose these enemies here had now a special check from our Lord and a command not to meddle until Mr. Fearing was passed over it.

Note that God gave ample grace for Mr. Fearing's weakness. Our God is not a cookie-cutter God. He knows our weaknesses and provides the needed grace if we will only humble ourselves. By the way, Mr. Fearing had no problems with humbling himself before God and man. Bunyan's lead character says that Mr. Fearing went down with ease into the "Valley of Humiliation."

Our boys regularly remind me how many differences are to be found in different people. Sounds obvious, huh? As a matter of fact, many of us miss this obvious point. Even when I think we are on the same wavelength, our boys often surprise me. Some of the times are humorous, but all of them offer needed instruction for their dad.

When our boys were much younger (five and two respectively), our oldest, David, was playing with a special train. His brother Chris also wanted to play with the train. Though David is generally quite good about sharing, he was not in the mood for exhibiting that virtue on this particular occasion. Observing what was transpiring, I turned to David and said with great earnestness, "What do you think Jesus would do, David?" Pretty wise, I know. I was getting ready for my son to have a massive epiphany and respond, "Jesus would have me share, Dad." But my son had his own perspective. Unfazed he looked up at me and said, "Jesus would make another train." My son was focused on the power of God. My focus was on the generosity of God. I learned once again that people are wired differently and I also learned the limitations of the "What would Jesus do?" approach!

So be leery of those who seek to show that every Christian's spiritual growth follows the same pattern. Don't let fancy PowerPoint presentations lull you to sleep here! We are created by a wise and loving God who gives us personalities that are truly unique. My struggles may be no big temptation for you. For example, my own battle with various doubts about the Christian faith may be entirely foreign to you. You may possibly have struggles that aren't as challenging for me. I trust that the "discuss and apply" section encourages you to see these things more clearly.

Discuss and Apply

In 1986 I had the good fortune to study at L'Abri in Switzerland. *L'Abri* is a French word that means "shelter." It is the study center that Francis and Edith Schaeffer made world famous. People struggling with all kinds of questions about the Christian faith find it a safe place to go. No question is looked down upon.

While I was there I got to hear more about Francis Schaeffer's own doubts, doubts that arose when he was a world-renowned writer and lecturer. Here was a man whom God used in the lives of millions, yet he himself struggled at times to believe the truthfulness of the Christian faith. During one period of time, he felt the need to go back to his agnosticism and work through the Christian life again. Like Peter, plotting the line for Schaeffer's spiritual life would show a time of going backwards.

What are your areas of struggle as a Christian? Who in Scripture encourages you to know that you are not alone with these particular struggles?

✦✦✦✦

Meditate on Luke 9:57–62. Note well that there are *three different people with three different areas* that keep them from following Christ. The first individual struggles with giving up his comfort, the second money, and the third puts his family before God. Which one do you identify with most?

✦ ✦ ✦ ✦

Remembering the uniqueness of each individual is crucial. Though talk on different personalities can arbitrarily draw distinctions among people, there are important factors to keep in mind. Furthermore, we must make a distinction between personality and character. For example, all Christians are called to love others. That is character. The outworking of that love will probably look different in a more introverted personality than it does in a more extroverted personality.

Another area worth exploring is how certain spiritual practices minister God's grace in different ways to different people. For example, all Christians would be wise to appreciate God's creation, but some may derive special benefit from taking a regular walk in nature. For those who would like to explore this further, I recommend Gary Thomas, *Sacred Pathways: Discover Your Soul's Search to God* (Grand Rapids, MI: Zondervan

Publishing Company, 2002). Gary makes clear however that certain spiritual practices like the regular reading of God's Word are nonnegotiable for all believers no matter what their gifts happen to be.

One happy trend (most aren't) is the rediscovery of the Trinity's significance for the church today. Some people think each Person in the Trinity is just 33.333 percent God. That's heresy, my friend. Nor do all the Persons of the Godhead add up to 300 percent God. Heresy again. There is one God yet three distinct Persons. The Father, Son, and Holy Spirit are each fully God. Each Person in the Trinity has certain ministries. That's diversity. Each Person is completely in harmony with the other two. That's unity. What kinds of practical benefits do you see coming from a better understanding of the Trinity?

Notes

Bunyan described the scene this way: I have smoothed out the quote to make it more readable. The version I quote is found in John Bunyan, *The Pilgrim's Progress* (New York, NY: The New American Library,

1964), 230–31. If I had to pick a book outside the Bible that best reflects my own understanding of what God teaches about spiritual growth, it would be *The Pilgrim's Progress.*

It still amazes me how many Christians have not read this book. Many Americans read this book up to the nineteenth century. Because of this, historian and best-selling author David McCullough said that it was "essential to understanding our country." Many accessible versions are available. There really are no good excuses to bypass reading Bunyan's masterpiece. One version that you may want to check out is Craig and Janet Parshall, *Traveling a Pilgrim's Path: Preparing Your Child to Navigate the Journey of Faith* (Carol Stream, IL: Tyndale House Publishing, 2003).

Chapter 2

How Larry King Saved Me

During the summer of 2000, it was my great privilege to interview best-selling author and adviser to several presidents, William F. Buckley. Buckley's weekly program *Firing Line* remains one of the longest running shows in television history at thirty-three years. My own interview with Buckley eventually became a television special that aired nationally on PBS.

You must realize that since I was in my late teens Buckley has been on my very short list of "those I would most like to meet." I recall watching Buckley appear as a guest on the *Tonight Show* with Johnny Carson. I was about ten at the time so I did not understand much of what was being said. There were simply too many big words and ideas. Both Carson and his audience clearly enjoyed Buckley's humor. Buckley's smart and engaging demeanor impressed me. Now in my forties my dream of meeting him was coming true.

Before the interview several people asked (rather gingerly, for they didn't want to create any unnecessary doubts!) whether I was nervous. For a number of reasons I wasn't, but a few days before the big interview I started to get a bit nervous about not being nervous! Fortunately, Larry King saved me.

I was exercising at my hotel in New York City. Larry King was interviewing the Dalai Lama. The Human Genome Project had made some recent discoveries. Larry asked the Dalai what he thought about the human genome. The Dalai didn't understand what Larry was talking about. Larry pressed the issue. Greater confusion was apparent on the Dalai's face. In broken English the Dalai tried to ask some clarifying question that didn't make much sense. Larry, ever the persistent interviewer, kept pressing. Finally Larry asked, "So Dalai what do you think about DNA?" How's that for an open-ended question? I kept picturing the blank, confused stare of the Dalai coupled with his rather incoherent response. I couldn't stop laughing. It was good that I was alone.

If "Mr. Talk" can get a bit stumped at times, then surely the pressure was off of me. Thanks, Larry! You saved me. I should add that I was very comfortable with Mr. Buckley during the interview. Later he had some very complimentary things to say about the unique nature of my approach with him.

Though Larry helped, what really gave me perspective was being aware of how putting celebrities like Buckley on a pedestal is another form of idolatry. That may sound somewhat odd or extreme, so let me explain it a bit.

There is only one true God. It is clear from the Bible that only He is worthy of worship (e.g., see Deut. 6:4–6; Isa. 43:10). It is also clear that we are designed to worship. If we don't worship the true God, we will necessarily worship something or someone else. Nothing other than God is life-giving so the worship of lesser things will end up destroying us (see Rom. 1:21–25). That's why God's goodness is clearly evident when He commands us to worship Him. It is not, as is popularly thought, because God is on some "ego trip." Only God-centered worship produces life. Every other form of worship produces death (see Pss. 115:8; 135:18).

You may be thinking that you really don't struggle with being an idolater. You pray, read your Bible, attend a good church, and enjoy Christian fellowship. You read passages in the Bible like Isaiah 44:8–20 and are amazed at how silly people must have been back then. How in the world could those dolts believe that idol they made with their own hands was worthy of worship? The leftover materials after the new idol was constructed were then thrown in the fire. This served to keep the idolater warm. What a capacity for stupidity!

Allow me to explain how idolatry looks in my own life. I am reading my Bible, talking with someone about God, or just thinking about spiritual matters. I start to ponder something God says about Himself or me that I don't particularly like. Did God really speak that way to Job? Am I really in as desperate a state as Romans chapter 3 describes? My mind begins to assess the "appropriateness" of such things. Maybe it isn't quite that way. If God could just be a little more like . . . Slowly, with my creative juices and carnal desires engaged, I have fashioned a new God. This God now serves me. It wasn't with my hands, but my mind was quite capable of fashioning an idol. Years ago John Calvin wrote of this particular phenomenon. He mentioned how our minds are constantly at work to create idols.

Other saints of old have talked about having "properly ordered loves." Who or what do you love most? If golf, shopping, travel, reading, or even your family is at the top of the list, your loves are not properly ordered. Or if you are like the woman I met in the pet store who was immensely curious to find out all about our new puppy but had no interest in even knowing our youngest son's name, then your loves are not properly ordered. When your loves are not properly ordered, you are engaged in some form of idolatry.

Let's look at a common problem to drive the point home. Recently I posed some questions to a friend on the desire to please others. His candid response was refreshing and not difficult to understand. After all, how do you think I came up with the idea in the first place? Here is what I asked him: how much stress and anxiety could be removed from his life if he really did not care whether people thought he was insightful or superficial, smart or stupid, kind or mean, godly or ungodly.

Wait a minute! Aren't we supposed to be concerned about our "witness"? Yes, we are. How can I say we shouldn't care? I mean not caring in the sense that we ultimately live our lives for an audience of One (see Col. 3:23–24). We need to be sensitive toward others and do all we can to serve them (see Phil. 2:1–8). We are told "so far as it depends on you, be at peace with all men." (Rom. 12:18). But our happiness should not be dependent in any way whatsoever on how well people think of us. People are fickle anyway and their opinions of us will fluctuate. Some people live roller-coaster lives emotionally because they are constantly assessing how others think about them.

By the way, my friend's answer to my questions was a sheepish smile followed by the admission that "a lot of anxiety" would be removed. He is not alone. We all struggle with this temptation at various times throughout our lives. Even heroes of the faith such as St. Augustine candidly describe their own battles with this issue.

May we find greater freedom and joy in living for the only One who is worthy of our attention. Anything else that receives our primary attention is not only idolatrous, but it will never produce life.

Make sure to take ample time to ponder the following questions.

Discuss and Apply

The passage of Scripture that God has used the most by far to help me with this issue of idolatry is Isaiah 2:11–22. In fact, I memorized and mediated on Isaiah 2:22 several times before my interview with William F. Buckley. God gave me great liberty and joy from mulling over that verse. It helped me be at peace a whole lot more than Larry King's gaffe ever could!

Take some time to consider this passage of Scripture. What strikes you most from looking at it? Consider memorizing Isaiah 2:22. I guarantee that it will help you see the stupidity of caring about what others think of you. You could say that this verse inspired the saying that "all men put on their pants one leg at a time." You may also want to look at Psalm 103:15–16 and James 4:13–14 to remind yourself of how fleeting life really is.

✦ ✦ ✦ ✦

It's been said that whatever "excites you most is God to you." Do you agree with that? Think about watching football, shopping, travel, receiving a major promotion, or enjoying a great sexual relationship with your wife. Is it realistic to think that God should excite us more? What does genuine excitement look like, especially when some people are quieter by nature?

✦ ✦ ✦ ✦

The last verse in John's first epistle is "Little children, guard yourselves from idols" (1 John 5:21). John wrote that to Christians. Take some time to read through the whole epistle. Why does John close with a verse on guarding against idolatry?

Notes

Years ago John Calvin wrote . . . *Institutes of Christian Religion*, 1.11.8. Various editions are available.

Even heroes of the faith such as St. Augustine . . . *Confessions*, 10.37.61. An inexpensive and reliable translation is the one by Henry Chadwick (New York, NY: Oxford University Press, 1991).

Chapter 3

What Weeds Taught Me about Christian Growth

When I slow down, I find myself learning important lessons in the most unlikely places. Believe it or not, the weeds in my back yard have served up (and they keep serving!) some helpful insights about Christian growth. My front yard hasn't taught me as much because very few weeds have taken up residence there. My back yard grows enough of these unwelcome guests to make them a fertile field for significant truths. Here is what I have learned so far (in no particular order of importance):

• Some of the big weeds are actually easier to pull than some of their smaller kin. Looks can be deceiving. For example, I have found that some non-Christians who were quite intimidating in their appearance were actually quite open to hearing about Jesus. The opposite is equally true. Others who "looked nice" were actually very antagonistic to considering the claims of Christ.

My adventures in arresting shoplifters prior to attending seminary might shed some additional light on this first principle. I quickly found out that all types of people shoplift—young and old, rich and poor. Why would the rich shoplift? One reason given to me by the wealthy son of a Hollywood producer I arrested is boredom.

Yes, old people shoplift. Your sweet old grandmother may actually be quite adept at the "five-finger discount." My boss, a former policeman, once arrested a sweet old lady, or so he thought. When he gently grabbed the elderly woman's elbow to escort her back into the store, she yelled and punched him. He proceeded to grab her arm a little tighter, but granny's punching got more vicious. Not only did it annoy him, but it was starting to hurt! My boss glanced around to make sure that no one was looking and commenced to clock her. It was lights out for grandma. Lesson learned: looks are deceiving. Don't judge an old woman or weed by its appearance.

• Certain weeds seem to grow best in clumps. They seem to thrive when they are clustered together. They like hanging out with one another. For example, you will find in reading Proverbs that "birds of a feather flock together." Fools tend to hang out together and the same is true with the wise (see Prov. 13:20).

• An obvious, but not consistently applied, principle is that weeds ought to be pulled out by their roots. Everyone knows that the old weed eventually pops back up if you fail to do this. Getting at the root of things is radical. Actually that is redundant, for the word *radical* comes from the Latin word that means *root*.

Even with this self-evident principle, it is all too common for people to avoid dealing with the root. Getting at the root of a problem is about as popular as getting a root canal. In business, at home, or in the church, it is tempting to deal only with symptoms. Symptoms seem easier to deal with, but they really aren't. When one does not address the root, the problem pops up again and again and again.

In business, it is called "crisis management" or "putting out fires." I'm sure you are familiar with how that works. A situation gets so dire that everything needs to stop in order to address the pressing problem.

During my years as a pastor, I called it "mowing weeds." Imagine that you are having a dinner party. Inside the house looks great, but the yard is atrocious. Weeds are in abundance. It is late in the afternoon so you don't really have time to pull the weeds out by their roots. Instead, you choose to mow them. It doesn't look too bad . . . for a few days. After that, they are back to their nasty former forms.

Like my dinner party illustration, some situations demand that the symptoms get addressed immediately. To change the metaphor, we know to put tourniquets on bleeding arms before making it to the hospital. Surgery will address the root problem, but the symptom also has to be dealt with. Never getting to the hospital to deal with the root of the problem is what too many of us seem continually bent on doing.

• Pulling weeds by their roots ought to be a regular activity. The roots don't get down so deep when we consistently attend to our yards. I am guilty of not applying this principle. Because of my allergies, I go out in the back yard on an inconsistent basis. I also have an "allergy" concerning problems. I'd rather not deal with them. Just like my physical weeds, I find that inconsistency causes additional problems. Avoiding the problem doesn't make it go away. Addressing problems as they come up (like the weeds) saves much heartache and work in the long run.

• Some weeds get so big that you have to break off the top just to get a good grip. Once some of the weed is lopped off, the rest pulls out much easier. This reminds me of the old principle of "divide and conquer." Some jobs are so big they must be broken down into more manageable pieces. I also remember the importance of patience when I see these big weeds. I must take the necessary time to do the job right. It's worth it in the long run.

• Some weeds are too prickly to pull out with my bare hands. I must put on my gloves. Otherwise, it is just too painful.

God's word is clear that we can't live the Christian life on our own. Like my gloves, the body of Christ provides a major protection. For example, when I am not sure how to deal with a difficult person, I am not left to my own devices. I can go to brothers and sisters in the Lord who will provide insight I don't have.

• Rain makes pulling weeds much easier. This is an obvious point, but it reminds me to wait on God. Rain comes when God deems it is the right time. I hate to wait, but I am learning how much God uses it.

• There is no need to attempt pulling every single weed in one's back yard. Weeds can be cleverly disguised amidst the grass. It is wise to pull the vast majority, but it should not bother us that some weeds remain.

This helps me to appreciate that perfection in myself, my family, my friends, my church and, yeah, even the world will not be a reality in this life. When I see a bumper sticker on the car in front of me that says "Imagine Peace," I am reminded that the sentiment stated there can never be translated perfectly in this life. There is a whole lot more to getting peace than simply imagining it. Once I noticed a car carrying the "Imagine Peace" bumper sticker and yet the two people inside of it argued with one another! I wanted to yell "Imagine Sin" but didn't think that would be much appreciated.

Take time to slow down and observe God's creation. The beauty, diversity, and immensity of this world just may hold some important lessons for you. It should go without saying that we must be wise to test what we're learning in nature by the word of God.

Discuss and Apply

Jethro gave Moses sage counsel about handling big jobs (see Exod. 18:13–27). What implications do you see in that passage for your own life?

✦ ✦ ✦ ✦

What principles about pulling weeds can you see at work in the approach of the false prophets (see Jer. 6:14)?

✦ ✦ ✦ ✦

Minor issues did not sidetrack the Jerusalem Council (see Acts 15:1–29). What allowed them to stick to the heart (or root) of the matter?

Notes

One reason given to me . . . I found out later that there are studies that talk about boredom as a motivation for shoplifting. See Richard Winter, *Still Bored in a Culture of Entertainment* (Downers Grove, IL: InterVaristy Press, 2002), 110.

I hate to wait . . . A terrific book on this critically important subject is Ben Patterson, *Waiting: Finding Hope When God Seems Silent* (Downers Grove, IL: InterVarsity Press, 1989).

Chapter 4

What Is Your Sin I.Q.?

It is fashionable to measure intelligence. The letters "I.Q." are a well-known abbreviation for designating how much smarts someone has. As with many things, the original understanding of I.Q. has been both challenged and expanded. Some say that the standardized I.Q. test does not measure other areas of intelligence such as how well a person can "read" others. The knack certain people have to get accurate first impressions of others is now categorized as a valid form of intelligence. That is why it is no surprise that books on social and emotional "intelligence" become best sellers. Some experts speak of more than one hundred areas of valid types of intelligence.

Since these things tend to take on a life of their own, I am sure that we are not far from embracing the idea that even if someone can't read or write, their "sports I.Q." is staggering. Another person may be quite a dolt when it comes to mathematics, but their "shopping I.Q." is deep into the genius realm. They have a gift for finding the best sales. Why shouldn't the uncanny ability to land a great deal on a set of golf clubs be labeled brilliant?

I would like to add one more area—"sin I.Q." Judging from what we Christians supposedly believe, one would think we'd have better than average quotients when it comes to this area of "intelligence." Tragically I have to say that many Christian books and sermons show a severe retardation when it comes to the sin I.Q. A low sin I.Q. results in a rationalization of our propensity to break God's commands. A "genius" I.Q. does not mean that we stop sinning. A higher sin I.Q. means that we are growing in humility and dependence on God's grace to sustain us.

Saul and David both sinned against the Lord. The case could be made that David's offenses were more egregious. When David tried to cover up his sin, his sin I.Q. was low. When David confessed his evil before the Lord, his sin I.Q. dramatically shot up (see Pss. 32 and 51).

I'll never forget one particular minister I debated. Judging by my sin I.Q. idea, he was severely retarded. He said that he had not sinned in ten years! I should add that he said it rather proudly. I read and then commented briefly on 1 John, especially where it says one is a "liar" if he thinks he does not sin. Preacher Man's response to me was anything but flattering. Among other epithets he hurled my way were "demon" and "wimp." At the time I wish I'd known one tactic for dealing with such things. In the nineteenth century, a rather rotund preacher came in contact with someone who claimed they had not sinned in two months. The beefy preacher, Charles Spurgeon, "trod heavily" on the man's toe. This was a heavy-duty object lesson.

Hemingway's main character in *The Old Man and the Sea* would rather "not think about sin." Santiago was distracted with more pressing matters. Like Santiago, many of us feel that there are "enough problems now without sin."

We all carry a large capacity for self-deception, one of the many characteristics of sin. The polls show that the vast majority of Americans believe they are going to heaven. Everything is groovy when it comes to the welfare of our souls, yet God's Word says that "the way is broad that leads to destruction, and many are those who enter by it" (Matt. 7:13).

Let's look at a rather extreme form of self-deception to make the point. Try and guess who wrote the following entries in his diary:

> These days it is fashionable to ascribe sick-sounding motivations (in many cases correctly, I admit) to persons who commit antisocial acts. Perhaps some people will deny that I am motivated by a hatred for what is happening to

freedom. However, I think I know myself
pretty well, and I think they are wrong.

In another entry the problem is clear to everyone,
except himself: "I have much less tendency to self-
deception than most people."

The individual is none other than mass mur-
derer, Theodore Kaczynski, the infamous "Unabomber."
Though we don't sin in "extreme" ways like Kaczynski,
we all are quite comfortable rationalizing our own sin.

Given what the Bible says about the pervasiveness
of sin, we would expect to find Christians quick to recognize its reality. Sadly that is not always the case. It is
even popular in some Christian circles to object to the
designation of being both "saint and sinner." The thinking is that if we view ourselves as "saint and sinner" our
"self-image" will be dealt a lethal blow, thereby rendering us less dynamic as Christians.

A popular book on "men's issues" is not the place
for plunging into the deep theological waters associated
with this sort of thinking. Yet one thing should raise

some suspicion about whether it is accurate. Church history and the Bible (look at what Paul says about himself in 1 Tim. 1:15) are littered with people who knew they were sinners but lived joyful, dynamic, and God-honoring lives. In fact, remembering that they were both "saint and sinner" is what many share as pivotal to growing in their relationship with Jesus.

Some of us may be willing to concede the concept of "personal sin." However, the ways we try to diminish sin's reality in our lives show how much farther we need to grow spiritually. A brief look at one sin that typically travels under Christian spiritual radar should illustrate the point. Or maybe it is on our evangelical radar screen, but we think it does not provide much of a threat to our spiritual lives. I am speaking of the sin of gluttony. You may be tempted to discard what I am saying, thinking gluttony is not your struggle because you are thin. However, the sin of gluttony can manifest itself in a variety of ways. It includes "a range of ways in which we consume food, involving inordinate desire and immoderate pleasure. One way to be a glutton is to be a 'fussy eater,' insisting on interesting, tasty foods or a wider variety." Ouch. Also, keep in mind that the "king" of the "all you can eat contest," Takeru Kobayashi, is not obese.

In earlier times gluttony was taken very seriously. One very insightful writer put it this way:

> Indulging in gluttony seems like a private vice, a "cute sin," a matter between only the tempted diner and the eclair. But undisciplined indulgence in the pleasure of food costs us more than we dream: it coarsens and darkens our minds and ruins our powers of attention and self-control, of sobriety and vigilance. It hobbles and confuses us. It makes us prey for another Eater.

It's ironic that we don't talk much about this particular sin anymore, especially with the large portions regularly doled out at the average American restaurant. And then there are the all-you-can-eat places. And how about the doughnuts and other goodies at church?

Oops! As Howard Hendricks likes to say, "Too convicting. Let's move on."

Acting like sin and its effects don't exist is a common occurrence in our culture. For example, many popular business books tend to reflect a rather naïve view of human nature. Their philosophy can broadly be characterized as holding that "information alone produces motivation." The belief is that we are totally rational beings who would never do anything destructive. If we are honest about the condition of our heart, we can testify to the bogus nature of this belief. There are times when we are quite content to do destructive things. We no longer care about the consequences. We may have gone down this particular "road" before, knowing that it does not end up very pretty, but that does not stop us. We gladly take the trip again. Information alone is hardly compelling enough to keep us from sin.

Even though he has some good things to say because "all truth is God's truth," Stephen Covey seems to fall prey to the misguided notion that "information alone produces motivation." In a PBS special highlighting Covey's massive influence on the business community, the interviewer asked the very question I wanted to pose. The interviewer asked Mr. Covey if he ever ponders the "darker" aspects of the human heart. It was the only time in the entire interview where Covey was visibly flustered. Mr. Covey dodged the issue and simply repeated his confidence in the optimistic business creeds that allow human beings to do great things. He never answered the question.

We desperately need to find the biblical balance on how Christians ought to view themselves. Are we sinners or saints? It is true that Paul calls the Ephesian believers "saints," but that includes the need to grow. And Christian growth is tied directly to dealing with our sin by the various means God provides. Read through the book of Ephesians. Finding frequent exhortations in Scripture to live godly lives should not surprise us since Christians still struggle with sin.

The message of God's love and forgiveness is much more precious to us when we honestly face our sin. Here is a memorable way to put it: "The desirability of God's forgiveness can grow only as the deniability of our sinfulness shrinks."

We couldn't make ourselves worthy of God's forgiveness nor do Christians have the power apart from God to resist sin. We should never get over these wonderful truths. Every day we ought to remind ourselves of the grace of God found in Jesus Christ and the Holy Spirit who gives us the ability to live much differently than our own feeble attempts at piety. Remembering that we are *sinners* always in need of grace will produce joyful, courageous, and God-honoring *saints*.

Discuss and Apply

Ponder these words: "Most Christians seem unaware of or are apathetic about the sin that remains in them, but whether they recognize it or not there is a 'living coal continually in their houses,' which, if not properly attended to, will catch their home on fire."

What are some strategies the Bible gives that help us to address the "living coals" in our souls? Trust me, the rhyme is purely accidental.

✦ ✦ ✦ ✦

I have often thought how men's retreats ought to have themes that truly reflect the serious nature of our battle with sin. Matthew's Gospel (see 5:29–30) gave me one idea. Jesus instructs us to tear out an eye or cut off a hand (metaphorically speaking!) if that helps us to live a more godly life. In light of that, I think it would be great to include plastic eyeballs and hands with the orientation packets given at the beginning of the retreat. These would be vivid reminders to take sin much more seriously. Imagine the conversations you could have back at work when your business associates see a rubber hand or eyeball on your desk.

What do you think about the graphic metaphor that Jesus gives in dealing with sin? What new strategies for fighting sin does this make you want to implement?

✦ ✦ ✦ ✦

During my radio days I interviewed musician and best-selling author Michael Card. He told me about a man who used to greet people at church this way: "You are a worse sinner than you can possibly imagine." It does not take too much imagination to realize the shock that came from his comment. After a pregnant pause, he would follow up with, "But God's grace is much greater toward you than you can possibly imagine."

Read Romans 5:17 and the surrounding context. Do you see why Michael Card's friend greeted people the way he did?

✦ ✦ ✦ ✦

Remembering our own sin not only makes us grateful for God's grace, but it allows us to show compassion to fellow sinners. Consider doing a study of what the Bible teaches on this issue. I would recommend that you start with Galatians 6:1–5.

Notes

In the nineteenth century, a rather rotund . . .
See J. I. Packer, *Keep in Step with the Spirit* (Grand
Rapids, MI: Fleming H. Revell, 1984), 130.

Hemingway's main character . . . Ernest
Hemingway, *The Old Man and the Sea* (New York, NY:
Charles Scribner's Sons, 1952), 105.

**Let's look at a rather extreme form of self-
deception . . .** Sarah Van Boven, "A Killer's Self-
Portrait," *Newsweek,* 11 May 1995, 38.

**It includes a range of ways that we consume
food . . .** Dennis Okholm quoted in Rodney Clapp,
"Why the Devil Takes Visa," *Christianity Today,*
7 October 1996, 28.

One very insightful writer put it this way . . .
Frederica Mathewes-Green, "To Hell on a Cream Puff,"
Christianity Today, 13 November 1995, 48. If you don't

feel particularly guilty of gluttony, consider the other six "deadly sins." The seven are easy to remember. Years ago my dad told me to remember "palegas" (pride, avarice, lust, envy, gluttony, anger, and sloth). Dallas Willard gives some extremely helpful counsel on how best to implement various spiritual disciplines in addressing specific sins and areas of struggle. See Dallas Willard, *The Spirit of the Disciplines* (San Francisco, CA: Harper and Row, 1988), chapter 9.

Here is a memorable way to put it . . . John Ensor, *The Great Work of the Gospel* (Wheaton, IL: Crossway Publishers, 2006), 31. This is a wonderfully written and wise book.

Ponder these words . . . As quoted in John Owen, *Overcoming Sin and Temptation,* ed. Kelly M. Kapic and Justin Taylor (Wheaton, IL: Crossway Publishers, 2006), 27. Most of the quote is by Kapic, but the "living coal" excerpt is from John Owen. The editors performed a great service by making Owen more accessible to modern readers.

Chapter 5

Don't Blow Your
Brains Out

We have all heard it before. On the first day of class, the teacher wants to make a good impression and set us at ease. As she goes through the various requirements for the class, the following statement is made: "Remember, there are no stupid questions in this class. Please feel free to ask whatever you would like."

When I began to teach high school students, I pondered this often used comment. I came to the conclusion that *there is at least one stupid question* and commenced to tell my students never to ask it.

I always encouraged debate of any sort in my classes. No problem there. Asking the "taboo" sort of questions (and there are definitely some at a Christian school!) was also encouraged. The only question I did not allow was this: "So, Mr. Moore, do I need to know today's material?" This is obviously shorthand for "Do I need to know this material *for the test*?" I told my students that everything I taught they needed to know . . . *for life!*

How about you? Do you view learning as valuable *only* if you can see how it directly relates to your work? If so, you will never expose yourself to important areas that will better prepare you to live wisely. Education is also able to have a profoundly positive bearing on your work. Unfortunately, Americans tend to value only what they can see as worthwhile *right now*.

We Americans are generally impatient, easily distracted, radically committed to a life of ease, desirous of quick fixes, and glad consumers of entertainment.

Our love affair with entertainment was brought home to me during a flight several years back. I was sitting next to a Pakistani man who was pursuing a second doctoral degree. This time he was studying anthropology at Johns Hopkins. His first doctorate was a medical degree from a university in his homeland. He was a most polite and articulate fellow traveler. When I asked him what concerned him most about American culture, he simply parroted some of our typically cited strengths—democracy, free markets, entrepreneurial spirit, and the like. I told him that he did not need to be fearful of offending me with any criticism(s) he might have. Still somewhat reticent, he started to describe the value that we Americans place on entertainment over education. In Pakistan, it is understood that getting a good education takes "blood, sweat, and tears." He continued by saying that teachers there are revered even when they are boring. The "office" alone of teacher commands respect. But this is changing. It is changing because we Americans are exporting lots of "fun stuff" like *Sesame Street*. Educational entertainment (a nice oxymoron) has made school children in Pakistan much more critical of their teachers. Big Bird and Kermit the Frog are certainly going to leave most teachers in the dust when it comes to creative communication!

Our love of entertainment keeps us ignorant, and ignorance is not bliss. I heard Stuart Briscoe relate the following exchange between a father and his son.

> <u>Son:</u> How far is it to the sun?
>
> <u>Father:</u> I don't know.
>
> <u>Son:</u> How far is it to the moon?
>
> <u>Father:</u> I don't know.
>
> <u>Son:</u> How far is it to the end of the Milky Way?
>
> <u>Father:</u> I don't know.
>
> <u>Son:</u> Dad, you don't mind me asking you all these questions, do you?
>
> <u>Father:</u> No, how are you going to learn any thing if you don't ask me any questions?

It is certainly good to admit our ignorance (something that the most educated must remember to do), but we need to be growing in our understanding and knowledge. An observation by Derek Bok, former president of Harvard, is worth pondering: "If you think education is expensive, try ignorance." Indeed, stupidity is costly. What you don't know will hurt you.

Winston Churchill is one of the most widely studied and quoted leaders. There are many things that made him a great leader. One characteristic not talked about enough was his voracious appetite for learning. He was a true autodidact (expand your vocabulary right now if you don't know what that means). With breakfast he would read nine different newspapers. He did not want a press reader "clipping or marking" the salient sections. He wanted to wrestle firsthand with the information. The process of digesting the material for himself was invaluable to Churchill. Churchill's curiosity and endless quest to know "why?" is an example worth emulating.

Before we get to some of the benefits that come from intellectual development, let's underscore something that shouldn't be ignored: the pain of learning. How's that for a marketing gimmick? Truly learning something about God, ourselves, or the world God created can be painful. We dearly believed such and such but, alas, we are wrong. This is one of the reasons why many well-educated people are humble. They know what it is like to experience the regular chastening that comes from being wrong.

Luke Johnson writes about the need for patience and the willingness to suffer if learning is to take place:

> The ancient Greeks saw it as axiomatic that to learn was to suffer. . . . Why that connection? *Learning* demands *suffering* because it is painful to open the mind and heart to new truth. Pain is the symptom of a system in disequilibrium. Physical pain results not only from the body's disease but also from the body's rapid growth or from acquiring new muscles and skills. Pain likewise results from the need to stretch mental muscles around new ways of viewing the world.

Pain is certainly part and parcel of true learning, but we need to remember that education is also a great privilege. One group of people who appreciates this is the Jews. The well-known and respected scholar Abraham

Heschel wrote these probing words: "It is wrong to define education as *preparation* for life. Learning *is* life, a supreme experience of living, a climax of existence." Jews believe that on judgment day one of the first questions they will be asked is whether they set aside regular times for learning! Now there's some helpful motivation next time you are cajoling your little Johnny to get his homework done!

Businessmen will benefit greatly from reading literature, biography, and history. Historian Daniel Boorstin said many memorable things. One of them was that "trying to understand the future without a sense of the past is like trying to plant cut flowers." Visionary leadership in business must be informed by the past, and that requires reading.

Guess who said that businessmen ought to stop reading so many management books? This particular person thinks that most of them are a "waste of time." Other books like history, biography, literature, and even philosophy offer a "better return on investment." Sounds like a stodgy academic, doesn't it? Actually, it is the counsel of none other than Jim Collins, author of

Good to Great. Now guess who picked a history book on Jefferson and Adams as the "Management Book of the Century, circa 2006"? None other than the relatively well-known business guru, Tom Peters, coauthor of *In Search of Excellence*.

John Adams said that business and one other thing made someone "a great man." Would you like to hazard a guess? Answer: reading literature. It is unfortunate many businessmen don't heed this type of advice. The busyness of getting things done and the seeming irrelevance of study certainly are key factors. Too many men miss out on the many "practical" benefits that come from reading in subjects like history, biography, and literature. Here are two of them:

- Great books expand the imagination. When one is able to see his situation/problem from a new perspective, it allows for fresh insight on how to better address it.

- Reading broadly gets us in contact with others who previously dealt with difficult situations.

This offers fresh insight for addressing our own challenges.

Wise people have a growing appreciation for what they don't know. Wise people appreciate the limits of their own thinking and experience. They realize that all people have "blind spots." To better address "blind spots" the wise invite people with different perspectives to be "conversation partners." They also read widely. Ideally the wise avail themselves of the opportunity to travel and experience the stimulation that comes from a different culture. If the opportunity to travel does not exist, it is easy to go far and wide by digging into great books.

Check your menu of reading fare. Put yourself on a healthy diet of history, literature, and biography.

Discuss and Apply

When I am invited to someone's home, I regularly ask to see the library. Sometimes they want me to clarify what I mean. "There's no library here, Dave. The closest one is down the street about two miles." Of course, I am asking to take a peek at the books they have hopefully read.

A library does not need to be vast, but maturing Christians are readers. I won't say how much one ought to read. There are too many factors to make any specific suggestion apply across the board. It is cause for concern however when I see large movie or music collections but few books. It also concerns me when there are books on the shelves, but ones of a dubious quality. A book like *The Pilgrim's Progress* is worth hundreds of lesser books.

If I came to your home, what would your library say about you? What would you want it to tell me?

There is a common misunderstanding that knowledge and learning make people especially vulnerable to pride. It is certainly true that knowledge as an end in itself will produce pride. It is also the case that zeal not grounded in godly character can equally fuel pride. Check out the misguided zeal of those who burned their bodies in 1 Corinthians 13:3. So knowledge per se is not the enemy; pride is. And pride can be found in a person of great learning or a person who is ignorant and elevates emotions above all else. John Stott offers his characteristically wise counsel: "Well, God certainly abases the pride of men, but he does not despise the mind which he himself has made."

A related issue is the so-called battle between the "head" and the "heart." Too many Christians dichotomize these two with the "heart" typically receiving higher priority. There are a number of problems with this. I will highlight just a few. First, the "heart" as the Bible uses it is not simply describing what we think of as the "emotions." Rather, it includes what we think and what we do (the mind and the will). In other words, it is much more holistic than we tend to think. Second, note well that the Bible speaks of learning as a function not of how smart someone is, but of one's desire to mature spiritually (see Ps. 1:1–3; Prov. 2:1–5; Heb. 5:11–14). It is unavoidable. Learning is integral to Christian discipleship.

Notes

If you think education is expensive, try ignorance. Quoted in Sean Covey, *The 7 Habits of Highly Effective Teens* (New York, NY: Simon & Schuster, 1998), 218. I worked through this book with our older son and will soon do it with his younger brother. It contains much "horse sense." As with all books, one needs to be wise in discerning the author's overall philosophy of life. For more on that, see chapter 4, "What Is Your Sin I.Q.?"

With breakfast he would read nine different newspapers. Stephen Hayward, *Churchill on Leadership* (Rocklin, CA: Prima Publishing, 1997), 72.

Luke Johnson writes . . . Luke Timothy Johnson, *Living Jesus: Learning the Heart of the Gospel* (San Francisco, CA: Harper Collins, 1990), 61. Emphasis his.

The well-known and respected scholar Abraham Heschel . . . As quoted in Marvin R. Wilson, *Our Father Abraham* (Grand Rapids, MI: William B. Eerdmans Publishing Company, 1989), 311–12. Emphasis his.

On judgment day . . . Marvin R. Wilson, *Our Father Abraham*, 304.

Historian Daniel Boorstin said many memorable things. As quoted in David McCullough, "Knowing History and Knowing Who We Are," *Imprimis,* April 2005, 1.

Guess who said that businessmen ought to stop reading so many management books? . . . See Jim Collins, "Book Value" and "The Classics." Both are posted on www.jimcollins.com.

Now guess who picked a history book on Jefferson and Adams . . . Go to www.tompeters.com and see one of the entries for July 25, 2006.

John Adams said that business and one other thing made someone "a great man." Quoted in David McCullough, *John Adams* (New York, NY: Simon & Schuster, 2001), 170.

John Stott offers his characteristically wise counsel . . . John R. W. Stott, *Your Mind Matters* (Downers Grove, IL: InterVarsity Press, 1972), 10.

Chapter 6

Storming the Castle
of Unbelief

Outside of Salzburg, Austria, stand beautiful and imposing castles of a time long past. One in particular caught my attention. It sat high atop a massive hill and loomed over the lush green countryside below. There is only one way into the castle. You have to traverse incredibly steep and treacherous hills. Taking in the spectacular sight, I wondered how invading armies could possibly make it up those hills. They are too steep for horses and men in heavy battle gear. Even stripped-down, warriors must have struggled to maintain their footing.

Gazing at the castle got me thinking about the nature of unbelief. I pictured unbelief as a fortified castle. And like the physical castle, unbelief many times seems too formidable an enemy to defeat.

It's understandable why trusting God is so difficult: we don't see God, the world mocks belief in God, and suffering can cause the most devout to lose heart. As Christians, we all know by experience what it is to vacillate between truly trusting God and unbelief. So how do we go about "increasing our faith"?

First, we must want to go up the "steep hill." We're not playing around. We need to take to heart that it is impossible to please God apart from faith (see Heb. 11:6). We know we are in a battle, and we take seriously the short span of time we are given to honor God. Ed Welch's words characterize the mood well:

> There is something about war that sharpens the senses . . . You hear a twig snap or the rustling of leaves and you are in attack mode.

Someone coughs and you are ready to pull the trigger. Even after days of little or no sleep, war keeps us vigilant.

Second, we would be wise to get to know those who consistently fight unbelief. Godly examples challenge and inspire. They certainly have for me. Look for godly men. Get to know what makes them tick spiritually. The late Bud Hinkson played this role in my own life. Bud was patient and compassionate with my struggles. He did not give simplistic answers to the things that discouraged me. He did keep pointing me to the sufficiency and beauty of Jesus. Those of us who fell within Bud's orbit will be eternally grateful that we did. If you don't know any compelling models of Christian faithfulness, you can always read about them in books. There is much wisdom and encouragement to be found in good biographies.

Third, we must have the proper equipment. Grounding in the word of God, empowering by the Holy Spirit, and encouragement by a community of believers equip us to go into spiritual battle. These things are like "spiritual cleats" that allow us to grip the steep hill without falling down. We can be steadied and go on the offensive against unbelief if we avail ourselves of the equipment God provides.

Years ago I regularly heard about the nobility of "charging hell with a squirt gun." This was meant to depict how courageous people attack Satan's stronghold even when they have no real weapons to use. Zeal was elevated as the greatest virtue. Sometimes it seemed like the only virtue. I always found this metaphor rather ridiculous. If I am going to attack hell, I'm not going in with a squirt gun! Give me a tank and heavy artillery.

Biblical zeal is always tied to what one knows about God. We must grow in our knowledge of God to know what truly honors Him. Zeal can easily be misplaced. We see this in Scripture (see 1 Cor. 13:3) where some burned their own bodies (incredible zeal), but it only served to show how terribly misguided people can be. God is certainly not honored by that kind of zeal. This kind of thing still happens in our own day. Human nature has not changed.

Zeal that does not come from a true knowledge of God will not produce courageous and wise Christians. Zeal without knowledge of God is wholly inadequate for attacking unbelief. We are wise only if we assault the steep hill of unbelief with the equipment God provides.

Discuss and Apply

All of us could be more intentional to "walk by faith and not by sight." Unfortunately, many times we hear that having clear and focused direction in our Christian lives is imposing man-made legalistic standards. What is the difference between godly standards and true legalism?

✦ ✦ ✦ ✦

I have seen many self-confessed Christians (young and old alike) fall off the planet spiritually. They were "doing all the right things" and all of sudden were no longer interested in walking with Christ.

It is telling to hear the comments from others who are shocked that such a thing can occur: "James went through Christian schools. Now look how he is sowing his wild oats in college." "Barry had such a dramatic conversion. He was tired of making money as a corporate executive. Out of his emptiness he really seemed to embrace Jesus." Barry devours Bible study and genuinely enjoys Christian fellowship. He finds men who truly care for him. They love Barry not because he is wealthy, but simply for being a fellow brother in the Lord. One day Barry doesn't show up for Bible study. And it is not because he is sick or out of town. Barry no longer wants anything to do with the study. He cuts off all communication. His newfound friends are baffled and struggle to make sense of things.

I have found a reoccurring theme throughout these types of experiences. Briefly put, it is that people get disillusioned when they realize that following Jesus is very much at odds with the American dream. The American dream says that we deserve "personal peace and affluence." God's Word says that many of us will be called to suffer. In fact, even a quick read of Scripture will show that the American dream was not the experience of God's people. Since the Bible is eminently clear on this, it is truly amazing that many in the church today fall prey to such a false notion. This goes to show how easily we can be seduced and ultimately deceived by our surrounding culture.

One metaphor I have come up with that may offer further help here is "the barnacles are not the boat." Barnacles are those sea critters that accumulate on boats beneath the waterline. They can make steering a boat more difficult because of their added weight. If left alone too long, they can destroy the hull. Flipping the boat over to "scrape" off the barnacles is a wise thing to do, but it takes time and effort. We American Christians are especially vulnerable to confusing the barnacles (the American dream) with the boat (the Christian life as laid out in Scripture). Instead of scraping off the American dream barnacles with all their bogus promises, we sail on believing that severe suffering is nothing we have to worry about. When suffering comes, many self-confessed Christians feel betrayed by God and become bitter. "I didn't sign up for this!" The

American dream barnacles have now eaten into the hull of the boat.

Suffering exposes how weak all of us are in our strength. Read Psalm 73. How was Asaph strengthened to embrace suffering and attack the fortress of unbelief?

Notes

Ed Welch's words characterize the mood well . . . As quoted in John Piper, *When I Don't Desire God* (Wheaton, IL: Crossway Books, 2004), 102. The original source is Edward Welch, "Self-Control: The Battle Against 'One More,'" *The Journal of Biblical Counseling* 19 (Winter 2001): 30.

Chapter 7

The Key to the Christian Life

You go to a conference on raising godly children. Expectations are running high as you've been informed that one of the country's leading experts will speak. You're not disappointed. The speaker is witty, articulate, and really seems to know his stuff. He passionately describes seven non-negotiable steps for raising healthy, God-fearing kids. Feverishly you try to capture his every word. There's no doubt in your mind that buying the big album of conference tapes is a good idea.

Fast-forward a year later. You go to the same conference with expectations flying high. This time another "expert" is speaking. She is also witty, articulate, and extremely knowledgeable. In the course of her talk she says that two of the "nonnegotiable steps" mentioned by last year's speaker are actually dangerous in raising healthy kids! Not only that, but she has three additional steps. You don't totally despair because her eight-step approach is easier to remember. She uses the word "children" as a memory aid so no principle is lost.

You are in a quandary. Whom do you believe? Maybe both are wrong in some fundamental way. You go away from that second conference confused and a bit disappointed. Unfortunately, if you are like many Christians today, you continue to hold out hope that there is some secret or key in raising godly kids that you still have not discovered. You console yourself by believing that it may be found by racing to another conference or buying a recently released Christian book that "everyone is reading." You may be interested to know that this is nothing new. In the 1400s one well-known Christian writer observed that "often curiosity and the desire to see new things lead people to make pilgrimages. They seldom change their lives as a result, though, especially if they run from place to place with no real change of heart."

Now there is nothing wrong per se with going to conferences and reading Christian books. We can learn much from them. However, the best teachers point us back to the sufficiency of Jesus. They give "practical applications," but their teaching is Christ-centered and does not give the impression that there is some new secret or formula that they alone possess.

My goal here is therefore quite straightforward: to show that Jesus is indeed the "key" to the Christian life. It seems simple enough. Unfortunately, too many Christians are chasing after the latest fad instead. We would rather have steps and strategies, fads and formulas to guide us in our spiritual pilgrimage. Seven, of course, is the most popular number for these things.

It certainly would be easy at this point to misunderstand my concern. Isn't it the responsibility of a good Bible teacher to give specific applications? All of us need practical tips for "how to" grow spiritually, and don't these steps and strategies help us in that regard? I am in fact a big believer that teachers of God's Word ought to give these spiritual "handholds" if they are going to fulfill their duties. We all need assistance in *how* the word of God works itself into the very fabric of our daily living. Puritan pastors, for instance, are wonderful examples of this. Reading their sermons you find that they gave many practical suggestions/applications on *how* to live the Christian life. J. I. Packer writes:

> The Puritans knew that sinful men are slow to apply truth to themselves, quick though they may be to see how it bears on others. Hence unapplied general statements of evangelical truth were unlikely to do much good. Therefore (said the Puritans) the preacher must see it as an essential part of his job to work out applications in detail, leading the minds of his hearers step by step down those avenues of practical syllogisms [or arguments] which will bring the word right home to their hearts, to

do its judging, wounding, healing, comforting, and guiding work.

A faithful pastor must give "practical" applications, if he is to be a faithful teacher of God's Word. Practical is popularly understood today as that which is "readily achievable." In other words, practical means little or no effort is required. As a result, studying the Bible more systematically, practicing the spiritual disciplines, and reading good books are not deemed practical!

It concerns me that there is a growing trend toward offering specific "how tos" without an adequate emphasis on the sufficiency of Jesus Christ. Simply giving mental assent to the importance of Jesus, as John Piper reminds us, is not something God takes lightly. Neither, may I add, is it adequate to mature us spiritually.

What I am voicing concern over may not seem relevant for churches who say that they believe the Bible to be God's Word because Jesus is regularly invoked in such places. Yes, Bible-believing Christians do fall prey to "losing Jesus" in very real and detrimental ways.

The best teaching on the Christian life will always draw us to the sufficiency of Jesus. Knowing Him gives us wisdom on *how to* live life in all its wonderful diversity—whether that be raising godly children, handling one's finances, or knowing how to be a good friend.

It is interesting for instance that many of today's "spiritual warfare" books speculate on various strategies that Satan may use against us. Think about this. If God wanted us to know (and He does!) how to deal with spiritual warfare, wouldn't He make it clear what the tactics of the enemy are? The question answers itself. One clear tactic of the enemy is trying to lead us "astray from the simplicity and purity of devotion to Christ" (2 Cor. 11:3), but *simplicity* is not the best translation. It gives the wrong impression. In fact, the apostle Paul says elsewhere that we are not to be children in our thinking, but in our thinking be mature (see 1 Cor. 14:20). Single-minded is what Paul has in mind. We are to *focus* our gaze on Christ. Principles for Christian living can be very helpful, but they are never enough. We need to "grow in the grace and knowledge" of a Person—Jesus (2 Pet. 3:18).

Thinking and teaching on this subject for many years helped me to conceive the following three approaches for Christian growth.

The first approach I call "Christ as Top Priority." We envision Christ as the first and foremost priority in our lives. We get up early and spend time with Him right away. Family, friends, work, and hobbies all fall in line as subordinate priorities. This seems pretty good.

It is wonderful to understand that Christ should be the highest priority, but this is an inadequate way to view the Christian life. It makes it far too easy to isolate Christ from the rest of our lives. After we have our special time with God, we then can be tempted to go about the rest of our day with little awareness that the Lord is with us. We put a mental check that we are through with our highest priority. We now feel free to go on to other, lesser priorities.

The second approach I call "Christ as Influencer." This approach is much better than the first one because it reminds us that Jesus should influence every aspect of our lives. Christ is not isolated as He is with the first approach. But "Christ as Influencer" still does not adequately describe what the Bible teaches about the Christian life. Christ is much more than an influencer.

The third approach, and the one that depicts a proper understanding of Christian growth, is what I call "Christ as Center." By the way, there is nothing new here! Consider an example: Christians who work "secular" jobs and want to minister more faithfully regularly say, "I want to integrate God more into my job." It is actually the exact inverse. The truth is that work (and all areas of life) need to be integrated into God!

You may be tempted to say that these three options are really meaningless distinctions. In actuality they are extremely significant. Words convey ideas and ideas change lives. Look at Colossians 1. Christ is preeminent. He is "to have first place *in everything*" (Col. 1:18, emphasis mine). "Christ as Center" reorients the Christian to live from a truly biblical framework. A Christocentric life will be a God-honoring and fruitful one.

I remember hearing Major Ian Thomas say that fasting wasn't *the* key to the Christian life. He proceeded to say that neither is evangelism, giving, nor memorizing Scripture. In his inimitable style, Thomas preached that even knowing Romans 5–8 isn't the key to the Christian life. Then with great gusto Thomas proclaimed, "The key to the Christian life is Jesus Christ." That simple yet wise message has stuck with me for nearly thirty years. Living out the reality of "Christ as Center" will keep you from being seduced by the latest fads and formulas that are being offered as "keys" to living the Christian life. For example, Dan Brown's book, *The DaVinci Code*, did not create a thirst for "hidden secrets." It simply demonstrated that books promising to tell "secrets" will always find an eager audience. Tragically, purveyors of heresy like Brown are not the only ones who try to sell books by appealing to spiritual secrets. Look at popular Christian books. Some use the word "secret" to capture a larger market share of the reading public. The carnal desire to hear about secrets sells books. Secrets also sell conferences and tapes, as well as offer a whole cottage industry of spiritual trinkets. I have not checked to see if there a book called *The Secrets of a Man's Soul* or something close to it, but I'm betting it exists. If it doesn't, I just gave someone a bad idea!

We must go back to the Bible. God is clear on this issue. The book of Proverbs gives us much help with the personification of wisdom. Wisdom is not removed from the hustle and bustle of life. Wisdom does not reside in some lofty tower where only a few, select people can go and then deliver the secrets to the rest of us lowly folk. No, wisdom is shouting "in the street." God's wisdom is accessible. Anyone who desires wisdom more than worldly riches can have her (see Prov. 1:20–2:7; 8:1–3ff).

Discuss and Apply

If Jesus has "all the treasures of wisdom and knowledge" (Col. 2:3), what does that *practically* mean? Spend time reading through Colossians. How can the truth of "Christ as Center" better be reflected in your Christian life?

✦ ✦ ✦ ✦

Why do you think "Christ as Top Priority" is so popular?

✦ ✦ ✦ ✦

I suggest that you read slowly through one of the gospels. Start with the shortest, the Gospel of Mark. You will see that Jesus is indeed *the* key to the Christian life. No religious fad can come close!

Notes

In the 1400s . . . Thomas a Kempis, *The Imitation of Christ,* trans. by William C. Creasy (Notre Dame, IN: Ave Maria Press, 1989), 166.

J. I. Packer writes . . . J. I. Packer, *A Quest for Godliness: the Puritan Vision of the Christian Life* (Wheaton, IL: Crossway Books, 1990), 116–17. Also see pages 98 and 104–5.

Unfortunately "practical" is popularly understood today . . . Quoted in John H. Armstrong, gen. ed, *The Coming Evangelical Crisis* (Chicago, IL: Moody Press, 1996), 63. The original source is Ken Myers, "Deliberate Life Together," *Tabletalk* 19, no. 2 (February 1994): 58.

Simply giving mental assent to the importance of Jesus . . . John Piper, *The Word That Kindles Worship,* in the Preaching as Worship Audio Cassette Series (Minneapolis, MN: Desiring God Ministries, 1998). You may contact Desiring God Ministries at www.desiringgod.org.

Knowing Him gives us wisdom on *how to* live life in all its wonderful diversity . . . Dallas Willard does a terrific job of reminding us that Jesus is the "smartest person" in the universe. He knows more about any topic than all of the experts combined. See Dallas Willard, *The Divine Conspiracy: Rediscovering Our Hidden Life in God* (San Francisco, CA: Harper Collins, 1998), 134–35.

PART
TWO

Your Relationship
with Family

Chapter 8

A Pooping Elephant Is at Your Dinner Party

Philosopher Peter Kreeft insightfully likens the big important issues of life to elephants. Diversions are like mice. We can be distracted from the elephant-size issues if we allow enough mice to cover the elephant. Kreeft says that a large number of these small creatures can cover our metaphorical elephant. As a result, we tend to forget all about the elephant. I like the illustration very much. I have adapted and expanded it to explain a common phenomenon.

Imagine that you are invited to a dinner party. The house is beautiful, the dinner table is elegantly set, and the meal is served in a way befitting royalty. One thing is at first amusing but quickly becomes very troubling. There is an elephant in the dining room right next to where your lovely meal is spread. Your initial impression is that this behemoth must have some kind of symbolic or hidden meaning, but no one acknowledges the pachyderm's presence. In fact, everyone acts like nothing is out of the ordinary!

Even when you try to make a joke about the absurdity of juxtaposing an elegant meal with a large mammal, no one at the table seems to care. Just when you thought you were sufficiently shocked, you find that this horror is about to take on massive proportions.

The elephant starts to poop. One does not need an active imagination to realize how "problematic" this is, an understatement if there ever was one! Still, no one at the dinner party flinches. The conversation continues as if there were nothing wrong.

One woman raves about the homemade croutons. They really made the salad come alive. Another guest compliments the hosts on how lovely the house looks. It looks so clean! The husband speaks up first and with thinly veiled pride says that they use an exterminator every month. "And they are an organic exterminator," the wife adds. You want to scream, "Who cares if you may have never seen a bug in your house? You have a three-ton elephant doing his business right next to us! Isn't that a bit more important?!"

It is easy to get caught up in minor things and fail to notice the big stuff. Even when the consequences for this kind of neglect are getting serious, we can remain wonderfully distracted. We all must face the "pooping elephants" before they stampede and truly make us have to take notice. Waiting too long necessitates damage control, and that is never fun.

A wise Frenchman, Blaise Pascal, wrote penetratingly on how most of us choose to get diverted by unimportant matters:

> However sad a man may be, if you can persuade him to take up some diversion he will be happy while it lasts, and however happy a man

may be, if he lacks diversion and has no absorbing passion or entertainment to keep boredom away, he will soon be depressed and unhappy. Without diversion there is no joy; with diversion there is no sadness. That is what constitutes the happiness of persons of rank, for they have a number of people to divert them and the ability to keep them in this state.

Pascal exaggerates to make a point. He is not saying that rich people are ultimately happy. He knows better as a Christian. He is saying that wealthy folk can keep giving themselves to various pleasures that hinder honest reflection about painful realities.

It is interesting to think about Pascal's point in our American setting today. Now just about everyone can hook up to the Internet and be "wonderfully diverted" from the painful issues of life. When sadness arises, you no longer have to be wealthy to afford court jesters for amusement. Go to the Internet and indulge in just about anything your sad, self-serving heart would like. Sure it kills your soul, but it does allow you to forget about the struggles of a difficult marriage or job.

We can now titillate and "satisfy" about every appetite we have from the anonymity of a home computer. I put *satisfy* in quotes because most of us are aware that these ungodly cravings create even deeper holes in our heart. Our media saturated culture gladly creates what I like to call "black holes of desire." There's lots of money to be made in the marketing of these pseudo pleasures that keep us diverted from more important matters. Imagine for a moment the tragedy of increasing numbers of people who will literally die at their computers surfing the Internet! One of my favorite writers speaks to the lethal nature of diversion this way:

> Society is a bored, gluttonous king employing a court jester to divert it after an overindulgent meal. But that kind of joy never penetrates our lives, never changes our basic constitution. The effects are extremely temporary—a few minutes, a few hours, a few days at most. When

we run out of money, the joy trickles away. We cannot make ourselves joyful.

One very helpful way to keep from being diverted from more important matters is being accountable to someone else. Roger and Warren are two men whom I meet with on a weekly basis for this very reason. We have been doing this since I first arrived in Austin some fourteen years ago. We don't use any prescribed program or list of questions. (If you want to use a set of questions to facilitate some structure, by all means do so.) Our times are freewheeling with no real agenda other than to encourage one another. These guys push, prod, and provoke. And I return the favor! Their love for me is unwavering. I view them as spiritual "speed bumps" on the road of life. Pretty poetic, I know. In any case, they serve to slow me down and consider what is really going on in my life. Like speed bumps for my car, I can choose to race over them. I always have the opportunity to lie and deceive these guys, but the jolts to my "spiritual car" make that rather unappealing.

You may have some serious business to do with God on this issue. I trust that the discussion questions help to clarify, convict, and challenge you to change.

Discuss and Apply

Dallas Willard writes eloquently about the "risk" of solitude. Time alone forces us to face issues that we are typically "too busy" to consider. Are you failing to "slow down" and reflect upon your life because there is an "elephant" that you are trying to avoid?

Years ago I heard a preacher say that it is perfectly legal to run a race in army boots. He went on to say it is not very wise and you will never win a race donning such goofy garb.

We are to "lay aside every encumbrance" (Heb. 12:1). Encumbrances are not sins. They are areas of life that are needless distractions and diversions. Golf may be one for some people; then again, it might not be for others.

All of us will definitely need godly counsel to help assess how we are spending our time.

Let me offer a personal note that might provide some further help. I read quite a bit. Nothing wrong with reading, especially the material I read (theology, biblical studies, history, literature, and books on culture). Recently I found myself praying about whether I ought to decrease my reading time and reinvest that somewhere else. Is reading as much as I do an encumbrance or is it consistent with my own calling? It's a matter that currently occupies my attention.

Dig into the Scriptures with a group of men and try to determine what insight God gives for addressing whether there is an encumbrance keeping you from running your race well.

✦ ✦ ✦ ✦

All of us are vulnerable to self-deceit (see Ps. 19:12; Jer. 17:9). We need others to help us address the deceitfulness of our own sin (see Heb. 3:13). Accountability to another person is crucial. Don't tell me this is unnecessary because you are already accountable to your spouse. I have even had pastors try to feed me this baloney. If you are really schooled in the art of spiritual rationalization, you will tell me that you are protected spiritually because you are "accountable to God." Sounds very pious. Indeed, we all are accountable to God and that is sobering, but it may not keep you out of bed with another woman. I am reminded of this when thumbing through my files. I come in contact with men (and some women) who said and/or wrote some powerful things, yet it did not keep them from making a shipwreck of their faith. God has given us one another. We need other men who lovingly offer their wisdom, friendship, and godly needling to keep us on the right path.

Are you accountable to another man? If there isn't anyone, start praying specifically that God would provide someone. Better yet, ask God to make you the right kind of person for someone else.

Let me offer a few final words about this area. It is not uncommon for pastors to get concerned about the lack of accountability among Christian men. This is obviously a very good thing. However, the remedy is not always well thought through. For example, I have observed churches deciding to organize men by zip codes! There you are with a few strangers to whom you are supposed to spill your guts. These "forced friendships" (a nice oxymoron huh?) are not the best way to have accountability. Are these better than nothing? Probably, but they can be counterproductive. Men may simply go through the motions and never really experience true accountability. It would be better if pastors taught *and modeled* this area of accountability. This takes much longer, and pastors must guard against getting too antsy. When the leadership provides a personal model of accountability that is compelling, more men in the church will eventually catch a vision for the same thing. The tragic reality is that most of us know how few of our pastors are truly accountable.

Allow me to suggest one way to "find" men who will be better fits for your own accountability. Simply stated, it is getting involved in a ministry that is consistent with your gifts. For example, if you have a heart for the poor, get involved in a ministry with that focus. This will put you in contact with other men who share a similar passion. I see men benefit from this sort of thing on a regular basis. I am also the thirty-year beneficiary of following this counsel.

Notes

Philosopher Peter Kreeft insightfully likens . . . Peter Kreeft, *Three Philosophies of Life* (San Francisco, CA: Ignatius Press, 1989), 33.

A wise Frenchmen, Blaise Pascal . . . Blaise Pascal, *Pascal's Pensées,* trans. by A. J. Krailsheimer (Baltimore, MD: Penguin Books, 1966), 70–71.

One of my favorite writers . . . Eugene H. Peterson, *A Long Obedience in the Same Direction: Discipleship in an Instant Society* (Downers Grove, IL: InterVarsity Press, 1980), 92–93.

Dallas Willard writes eloquently . . . Dallas Willard, *The Spirit of the Disciplines* (San Francisco, CA: Harper & Row Publishers, 1988), 161.

Chapter 9

The *Summum Bonum* of a Man's Life

Summum bonum. Impressive sounding, huh? These two Latin words mean "the greatest good." This can be a shorthand way of asking, "What is the greatest good to pursue in life?"

So what is the greatest good in life? What is really worth living for? Dying for?

Judging by the media and popular entertainment, a good candidate for the *summum bonum* could be a woman's body. The flaunting of a woman's body sells everything from beer to automobiles. As one of my friends reminded me, there is even a whole restaurant chain built around the female breast—Hooters. Marketing gurus are no dummies. They know what sells.

We Christian men have some major thinking to do in the area of sexuality. More focused thought on what God values prepares us to have a truly manly, or most importantly, godly perspective about sex.

First, we must admit that our views on sex are many times imbalanced. We go from one extreme to the other: sex as the greatest pursuit (or good) in the universe or trying to downplay our sexual desires. Either we indulge ourselves as ravenous sex fiends, or we act as though our sexual urges are really not that important. Both approaches are totally misguided. It is all too easy to drift toward extremes. Embracing extremes means that you don't have to remember other important truths.

Several years back I was officiating at a wedding. Everything was going according to plan. The service had the typical elements that you find in a Christian wedding. The couple selected a few passages of Scripture for the public reading. One was Proverbs 5:15–20. When one of the groom's friends got to the part of the passage that says "let her breasts satisfy you at all times," he left out the word *breasts* and simply said the innocuous "let her satisfy you." *Hey,* I quietly thought, *Revelation 22:18–19 says that it is very serious to add or take away from the word of God. God may visit him with a plague. That young fella may go home and find a bunch of frogs in his living room!*

On the other side of the spectrum, St. Augustine mentions how he once spent time thinking about the importance of sexual pleasure. He wondered whether it *alone* could bring happiness. Could he be happy if it was possible to have sex with whomever he desired, whenever he wanted, and without limits? One stipulation: he would have to get rid of all his friendships. In other words, could one be happy in such a situation as this? As Augustine thought about this self-concocted proposal, he came to the conclusion that he could not be happy. There was a pleasure that transcended sexual pleasure and that was friendship. In other words, he concluded that the *summum bonum* of life can't be sexual pleasure.

Prudery or seeking to satiate our sexual appetites as much as we desire are both deadly extremes.

Second, we must remember that God created sex. Don't rush by that! I am sure that you have heard this before, but it is worth thinking about again. The good and great God of the universe created sex to be enjoyed and savored within the sacred bonds of marriage. Read the Song of Solomon. A whole book of the Bible devoted to sex. If that does not get you to shout "Amen," make sure to check your pulse.

I received some very good advice on sex as a single man during my first tour of seminary studies. I recall one professor's teaching in particular. He mentioned how his teenage son was first introduced to pornography. His son had some "friends" who abruptly put a *Playboy* magazine before him during a break at school. Later this young man sheepishly told his dad about what happened. His dad wisely asked, "What did you think about what you saw?" His son told him that the women's breasts were pretty exciting to look at. The father wisely did not freak out. He simply said, "Yes, son. That is how God has created it. Your mother's breasts excite me very much."

One commentator translates being "captivated" by one's wife (see Prov. 5:19) as "staggering gait." I like this rendering very much. Our wife's beauty should cause us to wobble and lose balance. We should act kind of like a drunk. It is godly to be intoxicated with your wife. We should walk with a giddy delight as we consider our wives.

Third, some of you reading this will object that you no longer find your wife physically attractive. You think that it is impossible to apply the truths of Proverbs 5:15–20. There are a few things I want to mention, and you need to listen very closely.

Ask yourself this question: *Would God command me to do something that was impossible to fulfill?* Answers itself, doesn't it? God would be cruel to call you to something that was impossible. Actually it is impossible in your own efforts, but with God all things are possible. That's no religious platitude, my friend. I have seen glorious examples of godly men who love less-than-attractive women. That's actually not accurate because these women *are* attractive to their husbands. I know men who are passionate about their wives even when illness, advancing age, or extra weight brings change. They really look to Jesus and His love for the church as their guide (see Eph. 5:25–33). Our Lord loves the church, warts and all.

Internalizing the counsel of one very wise writer will change your life:

> If we were to look at the world poetically, then porn would too quickly lose its appeal. A poetic vision allows me to see goodness and beauty far beyond what the microscope could pick up. *But porn stars are impersonal, disconnected from my marriage history and my wife's sacrifices for goodness. In the poetic vision, the older my wife gets the more lovely and alluring she becomes because her history, sacrifice, and goodness cannot be separated from her body. Everyone would pale beside her maturing poetry.*
>
> At some point, this could get so dangerous that porn would actually look ugly, because it tries to strip goodness from beauty. In this

vision, we would have to worry that forty-year-old men would no longer find teenage girls sexually alluring because their bodies are symbolically tied to youthful shallowness and silliness.

Finally, stop being so passive. The world's system is opposed to God (see 1 John 2:15–17). There is no finessing this reality. The world is at odds with our Lord. Archenemies. There is no messing around here. Don't be a friend of the world. You will necessarily be an enemy of God, a grim and sobering prospect.

Too many of us Christian men are far too lackadaisical with the very things that seek to kill us spiritually. Don't be a fool! Things like your big cable package that usher you into the world of "soft porn" (how's that for an oxymoron?) are killing your soul. Wake up and smell the coffee. Better yet, if you are married, wake up and enjoy *your wife!*

Discuss and Apply

What are some other things that our culture tries to sell as the "greatest good"?

✦ ✦ ✦ ✦

If you are married, are you completely satisfied sexually with your wife? If not, do you think you have a "poetic vision" of her body? If you are single, what do you think you can do right now to be satisfied sexually with only your bride to be? If you remain single your entire life, how are you going to address your sexual passions? If you already have given considerable time to thinking about these issues, but are frustrated by a lack of clarity, I strongly recommend seeking out a godly man for counsel.

✦ ✦ ✦ ✦

The Jews have a prayer of thanks to God to say prior to enjoying sexual relations in marriage. What kind of prayer would you write for your relationship?

✦✦✦✦

Are there any activities (cable television, magazine subscriptions, etc.) that present unnecessary temptations for you? If so, what should you do about it?

Notes

On the other side of the spectrum, St. Augustine mentions . . . See his *Confessions*, 6.26. An inexpensive and reliable translation is the one by Henry Chadwick (New York, NY: Oxford University Press, 1991).

One commentator translates . . . Frank E. Gaebelein, gen. ed., *The Expositor's Bible Commentary* (Grand Rapids, MI: Zondervan Publishing Company, 1991), vol. 5, *Proverbs*, by Allen P. Ross, 930.

Internalizing the counsel . . . Douglas M. Jones, *The Mantra of Jabez* (Moscow, ID: Canon Press, 2001), 39–40. Emphasis added.

The Jews have a prayer . . . Lauren F. Winner, *Mudhouse Sabbath* (Brewster, MA: Paraclete Press, 2007), 71.

PART
THREE

Your Relationship
with Others

Chapter 10

"Narcissistically Wounded" Men and Other Screwy Ideas

I will never forget the conference call with a well-known pastor. My friend Roger and I decided it would be instructive to contact this particular man. I was a pastor at the time. Roger is a former pastor who now serves the Lord in the business community.

During our conversation the well-known pastor told us that all men are "narcissistically wounded" (hereafter NW for short). A short time after our phone call we were saddened to find out that this man left his wife for another woman.

This man mentioned NW as if it is a self-evident truth. Thomas Jefferson would be proud. At the time I was not sure I understood the implications when the well-known pastor talked about the concept of NW. Since then, a number of conversations and some further reading have given me a much clearer idea. And there are definitely things to be concerned about.

Some working definition of NW is needed. NW men focus on the hurt they've received. They tend to discount or diminish the hurt they inflict on others. NW men place the emphasis on their own needs being satisfied. For example, I've heard wives voice serious reservations over their husband's favorite hobby that might involve risk or danger. The husband responds by saying that he "needs the hobby to feel alive." What wife in her right mind would quibble over the need her man has to feel alive?

Some may be quick to dismiss my concern over this issue. Maybe I am guilty of insensitivity. At the very least I may be naïve to insinuate men have not been victims of real hurt and abuse. Allow me to address this concern.

First, it is clear that the sin of others and its nasty effects touch all of us. It does not take much effort to show that all of us are victims in some very legitimate ways. In my own life, there are certainly the lingering effects from the sins that people have committed against me. It is not necessary to unpack the details, but suffice it to say some were traumatic enough to make me reconsider the truthfulness of the Christian faith. Furthermore, I know others who have suffered greatly at the hands of unprincipled people. Finally, it needs to be said that this book is not specifically geared toward those who suffer from truly traumatic events. However, I do pray that they find this book offers a step in the right direction of healing past hurts.

Let's go back for a moment to the comment I just made: "those who suffer from truly traumatic events." This way of framing the discussion can get rather murky. What is traumatic to one person may not be to another. All of us have different personalities (see the chapter on "Stop the PowerPoint Presentations of the Christian Life"). As a result, we both process and handle situations differently. This makes understanding trauma rather challenging at times. For example, some soldiers come back from battle with burns and loss of limbs, yet they have no regrets about going to war. I have heard soldiers like these say that they would gladly go back into battle and do it all over again if they could. It can be hard for many of us to fully grasp such bravery. As a result, we may be tempted to discount such accounts of courage. We conclude that the only way soldiers can say such a thing is that they must be in denial. They must be suppressing reality because it is so painful. Though this certainly may be the case for some, it does not seem to explain all of the cases we hear about, especially when you consider the reactions of other soldiers.

Other soldiers come back with no physical injuries, yet they end up going through times of deep despair. They are plagued by nightmares and bouts of depression. No relief seems to be in sight as the hideous sights and sounds continue to haunt them from the battlefield. The pain is excruciating.

These widely ranging responses highlight an important point: different people process "trauma" differently. One danger with much of the current teaching for men is to assume that everyone is affected similarly by adversity. Again, the temptation in our highly psychologized age is to think that the soldier who is still eager to fight must be in denial. He must be suppressing his pain. If he doesn't come clean and admit some type of phobia, he will undoubtedly be looked down upon for his lack of vulnerability.

Let's stay a bit longer with military metaphors to look at another angle of this issue of "woundedness." Imagine that I go into battle where there is some heavy fighting. I get shot in the shoulder. The pain is intense. Fortunately, a helicopter quickly evacuates me to a nearby hospital. At the hospital I am coherent enough to describe to the attending physicians how my company of soldiers was ambushed. Some of my comrades died. Others, like me, were injured. Everything I have related thus far is accurate. It is exactly what happened. However, I left out one small detail: we were also gladly trying to wound and kill others!

Please don't misunderstand what I'm saying. I do think "woundedness" is *one* valid characteristic of sin and its effects. The problem is that it is wholly inadequate to convey all that sin entails. Making "woundedness" *the main way we conceive of sin* causes great confusion because it fails to appreciate the fact that we all are guilty of sinning against one another. Again, we all receive "wounds" from others, but we need to remember that we inflict our fair share of them! John Ensor has much wisdom and credibility to speak on this issue. John works with people where the wreckage of sin has taken a terrible toll. Listen carefully to these important words about a young man who committed a terrible crime.

> It is sad to think of a child growing up so unloved as to never receive a birthday card or a valentine. This young man was fatherless, and his mother was an alcoholic. Sitting in that cell was a wounded young man. But he was also wayward. I did not want to be scammed. To rape a woman is an immeasurably wicked act

of violence and an affront to a just and caring
God. Rapists *deserve* jail. Justice demands it.
I cared about this young man, but I needed to
care also about the well-being of the women in
my neighborhood. If it were not for the cross,
I would not have known what to say. But here
is what I did try to communicate to him over a
series of visits (later he was released and
I lost track of him). I told him that God is a
God of love, and therefore a God of mercy and
forgiveness. But I told him first that God is a
God of holiness, that he loves righteousness
and is angry at him for the harm he had done.
I assured him that God could show mercy to
him, but not until he saw how wicked and evil
his action was and how much he deserved to be
punished. . . . And if you will entrust your life
to the living Christ and obey him, trusting that
the cross is sufficient payment for your sins,
God will credit it as your own and will redeem
your life.

We live in a culture where too many men trash their families because of a sinful drive to "find themselves." Instead of acting like men, too many revert to, or more accurately, stay in adolescence. This should trouble all of us, for this kind of foolishness is costly.

Once again I may be in the perilous position of being misunderstood. Wouldn't God want us to be fulfilled? Hasn't God hardwired us to do something unique in this world? The answer to both questions is yes, but let's make sure we are clear on what all this means. Dying to our agendas and desire for personal glory brings satisfaction the way God intended. A media-saturated world is constantly trying to seduce us with the message that life apart from God is thrilling. We must pay close attention to the fact that "the world is passing away, and also its lusts; but the one who does the will of God abides forever" (1 John 2:17).

NW men are too self-absorbed to see the lies this world serves up on a daily basis. They are gladly being duped by a culture that will ultimately destroy them. What these "wounded" men desperately desire can never be found via the means that they have chosen. David

Wells states it well: "The irony is that this psychological hedonism, in which self is the arbiter of life, is self-destructive. Not only are we betrayed; we betray *ourselves*." St. Augustine said that his sin "divided himself against himself." This is a truth worth considering.

Sin rips and destroys everything in its path including the person who panders to his sinful desires. "Woundedness" is only healed by recognizing our sin and enjoying reconciliation with God on the merits of Christ alone.

A Special Word to Church Leaders

What are we to do with men who are cruel, insensitive, and uninvolved in the lives of their family? Many of these men come from long lines of abuse themselves.

The church needs to offer broader and more complete discipleship. The "discipleship" in too many churches today is canned and simplistic. Issues men face must be addressed honestly. This is one reason why faddish men's books keep selling. Trendy men's books tend to tell gut-wrenching stories about the "real stuff" of life. Great storytellers can get large groups of Christian men to believe just about anything that they say, no matter how biblically indefensible it may be. It truly is amazing how much bad teaching passes under the radar simply because the writer or speaker was so "funny and engaging."

Those of us who place a premium on thinking biblically are irresponsible if we only offer our critiques. Raising concerns about imbalanced or inaccurate teaching is indispensable to the health of the church, but it is never enough. We also need to show clearly what ought to be believed.

We need discipleship that is relational, covers the significant areas of life, and truly helps men come to grips with what the Bible says will make them godly. Spiritual oak trees will not come from superficial approaches to discipleship. This is evident in our churches by the dearth of men who offer compelling models of Christian maturity.

Church leaders must have a passion for discipleship. Pastors and local church leaders must both love people and have a deep understanding of the Christian faith. It's pretty pathetic that this needs to be said, but it does.

We need men who really "know their stuff" *and* have an ardent affection for others. There are far too many examples of men who "know" a lot but aren't very relational. Believe it or not, I've heard pastors describe themselves as not being "people persons." I have also been around elders who beg off on hospital visitation because it is not their "gift." You may go to these guys when a theological issue baffles you, but they would be the last one you would want to visit in a time of personal crisis.

On the other side of things are men who are fun and compassionate, but who have a very shallow understanding of the Christian faith. You would want them in the hospital room, but you wouldn't go to them with your theological questions.

It is clear that there is a diversity of spiritual gifts. For example, gifted teachers will be more studious than those not so gifted. However, American Christians have settled for an extreme between the "head" and the "heart" that is foreign to the Bible. We must remember that it is a mark of godliness—*not* giftedness—to study the word of God and the world He created. To further appreciate that, the book of Psalms is a good place to start.

I frequently joke that discipleship has "gone the way of the Dodo bird." The Dodo, you will recall, was a terribly ugly bird that went extinct in the seventeenth century. True discipleship may also look unattractive in many ways. It simply takes too much time. You need mature Christians who are willing to spend lots of time encouraging and equipping a few. It is not very glamorous, especially when many churches value the big, visible events. Get a lot of people in a meeting. That's where the real action supposedly takes place.

A Special Word to Everyone Else

In our highly therapeutic age, honesty alone can easily become the only virtue that is valued. Let's say that you are in a group with a few other men. One guy I'll call Larry takes a huge risk and says he's "addicted to pornography." The rest of the men applaud Larry's vulnerability. Being honest about his struggles frees up the other men to take similar risks in sharing their own sin.

The following week Larry shares again about his addiction to pornography. It seems to hold a creepy power over him. Again, the men in your group are affirming and genuinely glad for Larry's candor.

Week after week it never fails that Larry confesses his consuming lust for pornography. At some point Larry's honesty, though appreciated, is not enough. We should expect Larry to start making some progress (not perfection) in godliness (see 1 Tim. 4:7–8).

Look at your own men's group. Is there an over-emphasis on vulnerability that may be causing an unwitting de-emphasis on the need to mature spiritually?

Discuss and Apply

All Christians are given spiritual gifts. Study Romans 12 and 1 Corinthians 12 and see how a focus on spiritual gifts rather than "finding yourself" is the only route for genuine Christian maturity.

✦ ✦ ✦ ✦

Maybe you felt pressured by an overbearing father to be an engineer, even though a career in the theatre was much more in line with your passions. Let's assume that pursuing the acting bug is now totally irresponsible. The dream is dead, except for a periodic gig in a community theatre. How does remembering your own sin give better perspective to the sin(s) that your father may have committed against you? Is there a need to forgive your dad?

Be accountable to someone who will encourage you to reconcile with your dad. If your dad is dead, it might be therapeutic to make a special trip to the cemetery. If you decide to do this, I highly recommend having your spouse or a close friend accompany you. Forgive your dad as Christ forgave you (see Col. 3:13).

✦ ✦ ✦ ✦

Several of the men's books that concern me do seek to address an enormously important area—men need to have deep relationships with other men. Since God has blessed me with a wonderful group of loyal and godly friends, I tend to take this area for granted. I am also the beneficiary of older men who have provided wisdom, love, and a compelling model to follow. With all my compulsions and weaknesses, I would be lost if left to my own devices.

When we think of the apostle Paul, we typically think of things like his zeal, courage, and brilliant mind. We ought to also think of how much he prized friendship. For example, consider Paul's frequent requests for prayer on his behalf (see Eph. 6:19–20; Col. 4:3), his long lists of greetings to specific people (see 1 Cor. 16:10–24; Col. 4:7–18), how others encouraged him during times of darkness (see 2 Cor. 1:8–11; 7:6–7), and how much other men dearly loved Paul (see Acts 20:17–38). This is a wonderful study that may cause you to readjust your impression of Paul.

Notes

Listen carefully to these important words . . .
John Ensor, *The Great Work of the Gospel: How We*

Experience God's Grace (Wheaton, IL: Crossway Books, 2006), 99–100. Emphasis his.

David Wells states it well . . . David F. Wells, *God in the Wasteland* (Grand Rapids, MI: William B. Eerdmans Publishing Company, 1994), 14. Emphasis his.

Chapter 11

Some Dirty Little Secrets . . . about Technology

All around us the triumph of technology is evident. Technology is hailed as a savior of sorts. Even our conversations are peppered with language beholding to the massive influence of technology. When we don't have energy to do a particular task, we say, "I don't have the bandwidth." According to James Gleick, the inspiration for the idea of "*multitasking* came from computer scientists of the 1960s." Technology engulfs us.

It is undeniable that modern technology offers many benefits. Just think about going to the dentist a few hundred years back! I don't care for it much today, but at least I can get sedated so pain is virtually nonexistent. The e-mail I use on a daily basis still engenders awe. I can easily (and cheaply!) fire notes to our friends, the Butlers in Croatia or the Ryans in France. Many times I envision my various notes traveling at blazing speed over land and sea. It is a marvel to me.

Since there are many evident blessings that come from modern technology, it is easy to fail to notice some of the drawbacks. I offer the following list of potential concerns to foster greater discernment. And don't worry. I'm keeping my computer, garbage disposal, and flush toilets.

Concerns about Modern Technology

THE CONCEPT OF PROGRESS IS SUBJECTIVE.

It is common to throw around concepts like "progress" without pausing to consider all that they may entail. A thoughtful writer lays the issue out well:

Even with a definition of progress, its measurements and technological requirements are not straightforward. If progress is human happiness, has anyone shown that 20th-century people are happier than 19th-century people? If progress is comfort, how do we weigh the short-term comfort of air-conditioning against the long-term comfort of a pollution-free environment? If progress is longer life span, can we ever discontinue life support for a dying patient in pain?

WE ARE HUMAN BEINGS, NOT HUMAN DOINGS.

Workaholics tend to love technology because they can get more done with it. Since workaholics set the agenda for the rest of us poor slobs, technology's pervasiveness becomes difficult to challenge. Beware of the "early adopters" who make you feel out of it for not getting the latest piece of technological wizardry. Technophiles can wear themselves down to the bone. If you are not careful, you might be the next skeleton.

TECHNOLOGY MAKES US BUSIER.

Dr. Richard Swenson reports, "In 1967, testimony before a Senate subcommittee claimed that by 1985 people could be working just twenty-two hours a week or twenty-seven weeks a year or could retire at age thirty-eight." We now know how idiotic that prediction was. For example, the more contraptions we have to communicate, the greater the demand to return calls quickly to an ever-widening group of people. We're too exhausted to have meaningful relationships. There are just too many people to maintain contact with.

TOO MUCH INFORMATION, NOT ENOUGH IMPORTANT TRUTH.

I am certainly not a technophobe. I read several blogs every day. I also check the news and sports via the Internet. I do fear that the sheer amount of information is decreasing the discernment of many people. I find people believe things simply because some official looking Web site says they are. More subtly is remembering that information is not created equally. There are many bits of truthful information that are trivial and therefore of no consequence. The humorous point made by Thoreau in the nineteenth century cuts through the fog:

> We are eager to tunnel under the Atlantic and bring the Old World some weeks nearer to the New; but perchance the first news that will leak through into the broad, flapping American ear will be that the Princess Adelaide has the whooping cough.

Just substitute Princess Diana (or Paris Hilton) for the Princess Adelaide to know the same folly persists in our own day.

THE SPEED OF TECHNOLOGY CAN IMPEDE WISE LIVING.

The previous concern revolves around the quantity of information. Here my concern is with the rapid-fire nature of today's technology. Advertisements and our media-saturated culture demand that we make snap judgments. We live in a sound-bite culture where daily we are bombarded with thousands of different messages. It is tough to live a wise life when you are busy reacting to the culture.

JUST BECAUSE WE CAN DOES NOT MEAN WE MUST.

If we eventually have the technology for men to have satisfying sex because of advances in virtual reality, is that a good thing? There would be no more exploitation of women and no more risk of getting sexually transmitted diseases. Who cares if it destroys your ability to relate to real people? Just think about the growing chorus of folks who rave about such "breakthroughs."

I know you cringe at such a prospect, but it is a prevalent belief that the capability to do something logically leads to the conviction that it is the right thing to do. In other words, if we can create the machine, by all means let's get busy constructing it.

Discuss and Apply

What better recommendation for this section than slowing down to read a good book? Here are some terrific books that will make you think more carefully about this crucial topic of technology. You may even want to put together a reading club with some other men.

Brave New World by Aldous Huxley (many editions are available).

Well-worth reading, especially if you haven't read it since high school.

Technopoly: The Surrender of Culture to Technology by Neal Postman (New York, NY: Vintage Press, 1993).

One of my favorite writers gives a humorous and insightful analysis of technology.

Margin by Richard A. Swenson (Colorado Springs, CO: NavPress, 1992).

This is an extremely helpful work on understanding our relationship to time, cultural trends, and workaholism.

Walden, or, Life in the Woods by Henry David Thoreau (many editions are available).

Don't write off Thoreau because of his various excesses. This is an entertaining book that includes much food for thought.

Notes

According to James Gleick, James Gleick, *Faster: the Acceleration of Just About Everything* (New York, NY: Vintage Books, 1999), 168. There is a lot of fascinating information in this book.

The concept of progress is subjective. Alan Lightman, "Rethinking Progress," *Inc. Technology* no. 3, September 1995, 26.

Technology makes us busier. Richard A. Swenson, *Margin* (Colorado Springs, CO: NavPress, 1992), 148.

The humorous point made by Thoreau . . . See Henry David Thoreau, *Walden, or, Life in the Woods* (New York, NY: New American Library, 1960), 40.

PART
FOUR

Your Relationship
with Work

Chapter 12

Lose Your Job Every Day

Yes, you read that title correctly. If you are a Christian, you are a citizen of heaven (see Phil. 3:20), should want to please God more than human beings (see Col. 3:23–24), and believe that God is ultimately in charge of the universe, *which includes your paycheck* (see Matt. 6:19–34). Many times we are comfortable acknowledging that God is in charge of the universe, but when it gets to the specifics of our own lives, we tend to get uneasy.

Consider someone we'll call Robert. Robert is a hard-working, mid-level manager at a large computer company. His immediate boss is quick to cut a deal just about any way he can. He doesn't do anything illegal, but he is ruthless and never met a lie he didn't like. Robert is increasingly uncomfortable with this. Fortunately for Robert, he isn't asked to lie or pressured to participate directly in unethical business practices.

Robert feels the need to confront his boss, yet there is a sizeable impediment. In two short years, Robert will be fully vested in his company. His financial future will be set. Like Pumbaa and Timon in *The Lion King*, Robert will have "no more worries for the rest of his days." Robert rationalizes that the greater amount of retirement money will allow him to give more to missions, and so he fails to confront his boss.

Robert needs to remember two related truths. First, God really is in control of Robert's *specific situation*. Second, God certainly can take care of the situation without any of Robert's clever maneuverings. God doesn't appreciate it when we supplant His will with our wonderful ingenuity and scheming. Jacob's life is a good reminder of the folly rapped up in that approach. It is a constant temptation to rely on our human wisdom (see Prov. 3:5–6). Our plans seem so sensible while following God many times seems silly.

Robert is not alone. Ministers who are tempted to soften certain teachings of the Bible for fear of being fired from their churches are in the same situation. None of us are immune from these types of struggles.

I have seen up close the temptation many people experience to remain silent when disturbing practices are allowed to occur in their work environment. I have seen these situations play out in both non-Christian and self-consciously Christian places of employment.

Here's the fairly typical recipe for disaster: a power-hungry, manipulative person in a position of authority is allowed to exercise tremendous influence because those under him are fearful of losing their jobs. Also, it is more than likely that the autocratic person in authority has a particular aptitude or gift that is quite remarkable. For example, a tyrannical CEO is incredibly creative at finding new venues for expanding the business. He's a jerk to be sure, but his productivity makes everyone else willing to look the other way. The leader of a Christian organization is a prima donna, but boy howdy can he wax eloquent as a speaker. People are in awe of the leader's ability to turn a phrase. As a result, they tend to overlook or diminish the unscrupulous practices of the leader. Keeping in mind these dynamics, it makes sense why many dysfunctional work environments persist.

Another thing that makes these situations so difficult is the way we tend to make decisions. In short, most of us make decisions based on how we imagine the consequences going. We play out in our minds the various scenarios that seem most likely. The popularity of this approach is understandable. In fact, wisdom seems to indicate that we give *some* attention to considering the possible outcomes of our decisions. The Bible alerts us to the truth that what we sow, we will also reap (see Gal. 6:7). And what we reap typically has far-reaching implications so it is prudent to consider our decisions carefully. By applying Galatians 6:7 in this way, I have performed a clever slight of hand with its meaning so read on!

There is a problem with basing our decisions only on what we deem to be probable outcomes. Simply put, it is that we are not omniscient. Let's go back to Robert's dilemma. He has determined that it is far too risky to confront his boss. Robert has concluded that the loss of retirement income will be one of the consequences if he decides to voice concerns over the ethics of his boss. This is certainly a likely outcome. Then again, Robert's boss may respond favorably. Who knows? Only God knows what will actually happen, and therein lies the rub with Robert's approach.

It is impossible to have the clarity and courage to do the right thing when one is consumed with speculating what consequences may eventuate from a decision one is presented with. We need to base our decisions ultimately on what is right. We must trust God with whatever outcome ensues. If we don't, we will get overcome by fear and take the path of least resistance. And Galatians 6:7 is certainly not a proof text for determining whether doing the right thing is worth it because the consequences may be too costly. It does remind us that what we sow will eventually be what we reap. Robert sowed cowardice and he will continue to reap it.

Discuss and Apply

I recall one rather difficult situation with a superior (who humanly held my livelihood in his hands). I was given an ultimatum. I was told to keep quiet and go along with a rather unprincipled plan. Not too surprisingly it was cloaked in plenty of spiritual sounding lingo. I was alarmed for a number of reasons. It is not necessary to unpack why. What is pertinent is to see how a man who lived more than 2,500 years ago ministered deeply to my soul. His name? Micaiah. Not Micah mind you, but Micaiah.

The day before receiving the ultimatum my Bible reading had me parked at 1 Kings 22. Here is where we meet Micaiah. Micaiah was a brave prophet who was willing to tell the wicked king Ahab exactly what he did not want to hear. All of Ahab's prophets, some four hundred strong, were saying that a piece of real estate called Ramoth-gilead could be taken easily from the Syrians. Micaiah was the only one willing to tell Ahab the truth. He said Israel would be defeated in battle, which is exactly what occurred.

It is interesting to note that 1 Kings 22 tells us all we know about Micaiah. He gives the unvarnished truth to a powerful leader, ends up in jail, and we never hear from him again. Micaiah teaches us many valuable lessons, not the least of which is to stay focused on doing the right thing irrespective of the consequences.

Familiarize yourself with Micaiah. There is much to learn from this godly prophet. For example, note that Micaiah saw God on the throne (v. 19), in contrast to the false prophets who were enamored with the thrones of earthly leaders (v. 10). You will be heartened by Micaiah's example of standing strong in the midst of much opposition.

✦ ✦ ✦ ✦

The Bible has much to say about courage. There are wonderful character studies you can do: Esther and Mordecai, Daniel and his three friends, and by all means, the transformation of the apostle Peter.

✦ ✦ ✦ ✦

There are many commands in the Bible that tell us "fear not." The Bible warns us that the fear of man is a snare (see Prov. 29:25). What are some strategies Scripture gives for decreasing the fear of man?

✦ ✦ ✦ ✦

If the disciples were not afraid to lose their lives (see Acts 4), why are we so afraid to lose our jobs?

Chapter 13

Be More Impractical!

"Pragmatism," it is said, is the only philosophy America ever produced. Generally speaking, pragmatism traffics in the idea that as long as something works it is good to do. This may strike you as a bit confusing. We want things to work. Who would keep a refrigerator that no longer works? I am not contesting this type of pragmatism.

An extreme example of pragmatism is the willingness under certain conditions to rob a bank. Various surveys reveal that a large percentage of Americans would rob a bank if they could be assured they would never get caught. This is also not the type of pragmatism I am addressing here. I want to look at a few more subtle types of pragmatism.

Something that "works" is being used here in a specific way; what really matters is one's selfish desires being satisfied. For example, if a CEO is consumed with making money, he will not be concerned about putting a mom-and-pop store out of business. That is the American way. There is the power to do it so he will. It works. The only concern that may cross our CEO's mind is whether he is within the bounds of the law. Once he is confident that the legal requirements are met, he will be ruthless. After all, it's a dog-eat-dog world.

The business world is littered with pragmatists. A pragmatist does not lose sleep over employing unethical practices. He knows most of his competitors are doing similar things, and he can console himself with the fact that nothing illegal is transpiring. It's understandable why pragmatism in the way I've described it here is popular. Considering the ethical practices of one's business is far too time-consuming. Ethics raise too many messy issues. Ethics in the push-and-shove world of corporate America doesn't seem very practical. How many rich guys are known for being nice? Nice guys do seem to finish last.

I imagine some will object quite strenuously with my characterization of corporate cultures. After all, there are nice guys who run profitable companies. This is true. I happen to know some myself and am deeply grateful for their efforts. So I'll grant that not all nice guys finish last. However, even nice business owners can fall prey to various forms of pragmatism.

One particular manifestation of pragmatism extols various values. So far, so good. The problem is values are upheld not because they have inherent worth, but simply because they seem to help the company make more money. In his book, *Joy of Work*, Dennis Bakke offers a good example of this particular temptation:

> When a consultant from McKinsey was giving a presentation about AES [Bakke's former company], one of our executives asked

why he hadn't mentioned our shared values. It turned out that the consultant was enthusiastic about our values—for all the wrong reasons. "They really reduce labor costs," he said. "Employees love these values, and they work harder and more productively because of them." This is the pragmatic line of thinking about values that I had fought since the early days of the company. It ignores the moral dimension of values and regards them as nothing more than a means to make money.

Lest you think I am just going to pick on CEOs, pragmatism can be found among people from all walks of life and all types of work. No profession is immune. You can find pragmatists among clergy, lawyers, and used-car salesmen.

Even a trip to a Christian booksellers' conference in the United States provided me with many examples of pragmatism. I will share just one. My wife and I were guests of her publisher. My wife's publisher is based in Scotland, a critical component to this story.

One afternoon I was talking with William, the owner of my wife's publisher, Christian Focus. William was wearing a kilt. As we were chatting, an American sauntered up and started to laugh. He really liked William's creativity in donning the kilt. He gushed, "What a great idea to wear a kilt! What inspired you to do that?" William, who is an extremely gracious man, gently responded in his wonderful brogue, "I'm Scottish." The egg on the bookseller's face was enough to feed a hungry family of four. Sufficiently embarrassed he slinked away muttering an apology to William. Sadly this bookseller is conditioned to believe that everyone has some marketing gimmick up his or her sleeve.

One of the most probing critiques I've ever read of pragmatists comes from the former slave, Frederick Douglass. In his highly regarded autobiography, Douglass offers a scathing description of his own "master." Douglass says the "leading trait" of his master was "meanness." He had the atrocious mixture of being both "cruel and cowardly." Maybe the most pathetic part of the portrait Douglass gives of his master is this: "Having no resources within himself, he was compelled to be the copyist of many, and being such, he was forever the victim of inconsistency; and of consequence he was an object of contempt, and was held as such even by his slaves."

Pragmatists are held hostage by any number of external factors. In politics, the stereotypical pragmatist makes decisions according to what the latest opinion poll tells him. As the polls change, so does the pragmatic politician. It is no surprise then that pragmatists are what Douglass described as victims of inconsistency. They do only what seems expedient at the moment. The portrait that Frederick Douglass painted of his slave owner can easily apply to any pragmatist. Remember, the pragmatist has no inner compass guiding him. Like Douglass said, he has "no resources within himself."

The *rationale* of nineteenth-century slave owners is no different than many businessmen today. Slavery was legal, slaves increased productivity, and slaves provided greater profits. According to these pragmatists you would be an ignoramus not to exploit the material benefits that come from enslaving others. Today it's really not much different. Making sure something passes muster legally seems to be the only thing many shrewd businessmen are interested in finding out before proceeding forward in conducting their work.

Don't be held captive to the dominant way of American thinking that says, "As long as something works, it is good to do." Expedience may get you accolades in the business community, but there is a price to be paid. The Enron scandal showed us this in living color. Enron's undoing was not just that the financial status was misrepresented to the public. We also learned about a culture of arrogance placing little value on ethical concerns. Thank God for Sherron Watkins, the so-called Enron whistleblower. She certainly has resources within herself. Therefore she was able to do the right thing. It is unfortunate that people like Sherron Watkins are so rare.

The late Henri Nouwen understood better than most how "impracticality" finds favor with God. Nouwen taught at Notre Dame, Yale, and Harvard. He left academia to minister among retarded adults at the Daybreak community outside of Toronto. Philip Yancey wrote about his visit with Nouwen:

After lunch we celebrated a special
Eucharist for Adam, the young man Nouwen
looked after. With solemnity, but also a twinkle
in his eye, Nouwen led the liturgy in honor of
Adam's twenty-sixth birthday. Unable to talk,
walk, or dress himself, profoundly retarded,
Adam gave no sign of comprehension. He
seemed to recognize, at least, that his family
had come. He drooled throughout the cer-
emony and grunted loudly a few times.

Later Nouwen told me it took him nearly
two hours to prepare Adam each day. Bathing
and shaving him, brushing his teeth, comb-
ing his hair, guiding his hand as he tried to eat
breakfast—these simple, repetitive acts
had become for him almost like an hour of
meditation.

Yancey then confessed his own skepticism over
whether Nouwen used his time wisely:

I must admit I had a fleeting doubt as
to whether this was the best use of the busy

priest's time. Could not someone else take over the manual chores? When I cautiously broached the subject with Nouwen himself, he informed me that I had completely misinterpreted him. "I am not giving up anything," he insisted. "It is I, not Adam, who gets the main benefit from our friendship."

I encourage you to go out and be one of those rare, "impractical" businessmen.

Discuss and Apply

What is the difference between a shrewd person (see Matt. 10:16) and a pragmatist? (I am grateful to my friend David Drell for helping to think through this difference in ways that he didn't even know about!)

✦ ✦ ✦ ✦

How does John 6 show that Jesus was not a pragmatist?

✦ ✦ ✦ ✦

When it comes to leadership development, pragma-tists believe that the emphasis ought to be on learning certain skills. Character tends to get neglected. Study Acts 8:9–24. How is Simon Magus a cautionary tale in this regard? Also, read Acts 19:11–16.

This seems like a good place to share "Moore's Law of Leadership." This law states that as the number of books on leadership increases, the number of true leaders decreases. "Wait a second," you object. I am confusing correlation with causation. The increase in leadership books is not *causing* a lack of leaders. You, of course, would be correct to register the complaint. However, I do find it rather curious that there is so much talk about the dearth of leaders amidst a market glutted with leader-ship books. I believe it suggests learning some skills, even helpful ones, does not produce leaders. Churchill did not become a leader from reading books on leadership!

Notes

In his book, *Joy at Work* **...** Much more about the perils of pragmatism can be found in Dennis Bakke, *Joy at Work* (Seattle, WA: PVG, 2005), 32–33, 40, 189–91. I am grateful to my friend, Danny Smith, for giving me a copy of this provocative book. Danny is one of those "impractical" CEOs who upholds values simply because it is the right thing to do.

One of the most probing critiques ... Frederick Douglass, *Narrative of the Life of Frederick Douglass, an American Slave,* introduction by William Mackey Jr. (New York, NY: Barnes & Noble Books, 2002), 69.

The late Henri Nouwen understood ... Philip Yancey, "The Holy Inefficiency of Henri Nouwen," *Christianity Today*, 9 December 1996, 80.

PART
FIVE

Your Relationship
with Time

Chapter 14

Start Slow and Taper

I was twenty-six, single, goal-oriented, a college convert to Christianity, and a recent graduate of seminary. I also was the new campus director for Campus Crusade for Christ at Stanford University. Campus Crusade is a ministry I appreciate to this day, but one that tends to attract type-A personalities.

I met Brian Morgan during my first week on campus. At that time Brian was the college minister for Peninsula Bible Church in Palo Alto, California. Brian was thirty-six and in his last year of working with college students at Stanford. He is to this day one of my favorite Bible teachers. Brian introduced himself with the oddest counsel I have ever received. After the typical pleasantries were exchanged, Brian said, "Keep this bit of advice I received years ago, Dave: 'Start slow and taper.'" Though Brian exaggerated to make his point, I failed to appreciate the wisdom in it. I concluded (quite erroneously) he must be a spiritual slacker of sorts. You know, a "let go and let God" type who is simply justifying his own lack of zeal. I was all about building God's kingdom—go, go, go. Or maybe I was trying to build my own kingdom. In any case, the idea of slowing down was anathema to me. It was a few years later that God graciously taught me how misguided my view was about ministry.

While I was at Stanford University, I greatly desired to start a Bible study in the Sigma Chi fraternity house. There were a number of reasons why I felt this was a good idea. The problem was that I couldn't get anything going. After trying in vain for over a year, my "God-given opportunity disguised as a hassle" happened one day—a day I will never forget.

It was a beautiful spring day. I eagerly headed to the campus post office before the hordes of students converged on it after the last morning class period. As I made my way across the plaza en route to the post office, I heard a traveling evangelist on the free-speech platform. He was one of those "evangelists" who points out specific sins in the lives of people he has never met. Equally audacious was his claim of being free from sin himself! (He is the one I mention in "What Is Your Sin I.Q.?") To say the least, my spirit was provoked. I believed that God was telling me to go over and ask him some questions. Here's where I reminded God that this did not fit into my priority of getting my precious packages mailed. Note well the use of the word "my." In any case, I told God, "Sorry. I'm not available to interact with this yahoo. Ask someone else. You certainly can get the attention of someone other than me." God, however, was not through with me. After arguing with the Lord for about five minutes, I finally caved in. I went over and engaged this man on various issues related to the gospel. A crowd of several hundred students gathered and listened to our conversation. After our give and take was over, a student approached me about the possibility of participating in a debate that evening with my preacher friend. Guess who approached me? None other than the president of the Sigma Chi fraternity house! I didn't need to consider the invitation. I was elated for the opportunity. After the debate several students asked rather sheepishly if I would ever be interested in leading a Bible study in their house.

The study in Ecclesiastes with the men of the Sigma Chi house was one of the highlights of my five years at Stanford. Many times I got back to my apartment at one or two in the morning because these young men wanted to talk more. Two of the men in that study eventually became medical doctors. At the beginning of the study neither were convinced that abortion was always wrong. Gradually both came to see abortion as biblically indefensible. That's just some of the fruit that came out of the study.

Back to my packages that I was trying frantically to mail. Those packages ended up getting sent out a few days later. Was I upset that sending my precious packages on time got thwarted? No way. In fact, I don't remember what I was mailing or who was on the receiving end. What I will never forget are the godly convictions that were forged in that Bible study. I learned that slowing down to hear God could lead to ministry that gets overlooked when we are rushing through life. Brian was right after all. His somewhat tongue-in-cheek remark included a gem of sage counsel.

Discuss and Apply

God made the night and called it good (see Gen. 1:14, 18). Keep in mind that this was before the fall. The psalmist informs us that the night was created for nocturnal animals to look for food, not diurnal animals to be workaholics for Jesus (see Pss. 104:19–23; 127:2). Work through the implications of these passages and consider how much you "burn the midnight oil." Yours truly is still learning much about this area.

✦ ✦ ✦ ✦

Discuss the following quote with a friend:

Good sleep is one mark of the person who lives in the rhythm of Yahweh's giving and calling. Transgressing the limits of environmental rhythms can be an act of unbelief, reliance upon human works rather than on God's provision.

✦ ✦ ✦ ✦

Do a study of Ephesians 5:15–16. Warning: the biblical view of time is very much at odds with the way most Americans conceive of it. Make sure you ponder the implications of Ecclesiastes 3:1–14 as well. What practical insights do you think these verses should have on your own understanding of time?

✦ ✦ ✦ ✦

In Exodus 14:14 we find these penetrating words: "The Lord will fight for you while you keep silent." Make sure to familiarize yourself with the broader context. How well did the children of Israel learn that truth? How well are you learning it?

Notes

While I was at Stanford . . . This story is adapted from my booklet, *Confident Living: How to Discover God's Will for Your Life* (Austin, TX: Two Cities Ministries, 2000). This booklet is available at www. twocities.org.

Discuss the following quote . . . Quoted in Robert Banks, *The Tyranny of Time* (Downers Grove, IL: InterVarsity Press, 1983), 183.

Chapter 15

Let's Start a Napping Club

I enjoyed my time teaching high school students. I taught at a very academic and competitive school. It was typical to see the juniors and seniors come in absolutely exhausted. They would stay up late studying, start the new day early in the morning, and slink to their desks like zombies.

I decided this was not a great way to get an education. I asked how many of them were helped by napping. Almost all answered in the affirmative. I then proceeded to instruct them to put their heads down or lie on the floor. Those who did not like to nap had to be quiet. The lights went out for about fifteen minutes. Most of the students immediately went to sleep. Muhammad Ali famously said he was so fast he could hit the bed before the lights went out. These students were almost as fast falling asleep once I flipped the light switch.

I did not do this in every class, though it would not have been difficult to justify. It graphically reminded me how most Americans, and that certainly includes just about all high school students, are lacking in sleep.

I told my students that it would be great to start a napping club. I would gladly be the faculty sponsor. One goal among others would be to drum up some peer pressure for napping. When a pro-napping student engaged with a fellow student who felt guilty about napping, the advocate for napping was to exclaim, "What? You are not a napper! Napping is a sign of greatness."

When it comes to napping, my family is evenly divided. I derive a lot of benefit from a good nap, as does our oldest son. My wife and our younger son don't get refreshed from napping. Not all people are rejuvenated from napping. I feel sorry for them, but my beef is not with those folks. Rather, it is with those who see napping as a sign of indolence. There is no doubt this can be the case. The book of Proverbs makes that clear. However, the rest of the Bible includes examples (see the life of Elijah) and instruction (see Ps. 127) that underscore the importance of rest. As mentioned in another chapter, a lack of rest may reveal who we think is really sovereign. The children of Israel struggled to learn this with God's provisions of manna and the Sabbath.

There is an illustrious group of nappers: Leonardo da Vinci, Thomas Edison, Winston Churchill, John F. Kennedy, even my favorite newscaster, Jim Lehrer, to name just a few. Churchill had wise words for an American businessman who worked the typical 8-to-5:30 schedule:

> My dear man, you don't mean it. That is the most perfect prescription for a short life that I've ever heard. . . . Don't think you will be doing less work because you sleep during the day. That's a foolish notion held by people

who have no imagination. You will be able to accomplish more. You get two days in one—well, at least one and a half, I'm sure. When the war started, I *had* to sleep during the day because it was the only way I could cope with my responsibilities.

"No imagination" is certainly an exaggeration and a bit harsh, but Churchill makes a point worth considering.

Discuss and Apply

There is a great need to think through this issue of rest. And ministers aren't always the best people to teach us. As a pastor I typically worked fifty, many times sixty hours a week, yet I was the "slacker" on our pastoral team. Many of those guys put in seventy or more hours. It is no wonder a minister is responsible for coining the word "workaholic." Here is one of the many examples that could be given:

When Robert Murray McCheyne, the saintly young Scottish minister, lay dying at the age of twenty-nine, he turned to a friend who was sitting with him and said: "God gave me a message to deliver and a horse to ride. Alas, I have killed the horse and now I cannot deliver the message." J. Oswald Sanders adds: There is no virtue in flogging the tired horse to death.

How do you determine what is an appropriate amount of time to devote at work?

✦ ✦ ✦ ✦

A verse from Psalm 127 is briefly alluded to in the "Start Slow and Taper" chapter. Now is the time to meditate and mull over the implications of that wonderful psalm.

Notes

It graphically reminded me how most Americans . . . One study showed that most workers would sleep if they were granted an extra hour a day. See Leland Ryken, *Work and Leisure in Christian Perspective* (Portland, OR:

Multnomah Press, 1987), 45. This book is extremely helpful for thinking more carefully about this crucial issue.

Churchill had wise words . . . As quoted in Steven F. Hayward, *Churchill on Leadership* (Rocklin, CA: Prima Publishing, 1997), 125. Emphasis his.

Consider that a minister coined the word "workaholic." I am indebted to James Gleick, *Faster: The Acceleration of Just About Everything* (New York, NY: Vintage Books, 1999), 153. Wayne Oates is the minister, and his book that coined the term is *Confessions of a Workaholic* (Nashville, TN: Abingdon Press, 1971).

Here is one of the many examples that could be given . . . As quoted in J. Oswald Sanders, *Spiritual Leadership* (Chicago, IL: Moody Press, 1980), 176.

PART
SIX

Your Relationship
with Things

Chapter 16

Buckets of Beautiful Golf Balls

Something caught my attention during several visits to Florida. Wealthy folks in their retirement years collect golf balls from the errant shots of others. These wealthy people fill up large, white buckets with their newfound treasures and proceed to store their growing collections in their respective garages.

Since they are wealthy, they don't do this because of an inability to buy new golf balls. Collecting golf balls is also not for the purpose of having plenty of practice balls. In fact, I have never seen any of these folks hit their own practice balls. They hit golf balls at the local range because there really are no good places nearby to hit one's own golf balls. So why do these folks in their "twilight years" collect so many extra golf balls?

The answer may not be that mysterious. Collecting golf balls provides a nice diversion, and what's the harm? Older men and women should get regular exercise so why not double up and collect some golf balls along the way? It seems innocent enough.

Or could it be that the seemingly harmless diversion of collecting golf balls masks a larger problem? If in our affluent retirement communities large groups of folks were snorting cocaine, we would have cause to be worried. That is clearly a dangerous (and illegal) diversion. People take drugs to escape a whole host of things: past and present hurts, various phobias, insecurities, and the fear of facing one's own mortality. Maybe collecting golf balls is done for similar reasons.

Think about this for a minute: It is the funeral of an elderly man. He made a lot of money but was estranged from his only child. The old man was a master at rationalizing his neglect of the family. With a fair bit of reluctance, the son accepts the opportunity to eulogize his father. The awkwardness of the moment is palpable. The son struggles to find something good to say about his father. After stating some of the factual details of his father's business "success," the son closes by saying that it will be nice to inherit the nine large buckets of golf balls. "Thanks Dad," the son closes, "for taking advantage of someone else's slice."

On one hand all sane folks will agree that people are much more important than things. In fact, the comparison is rather silly because people are created in the image of God. Material stuff is a category all its own. Things only have value because we assign a relative worth to them. The worth of things obviously changes depending on a number of factors, most notably our interest in them. People have inherent worth. Our worth never changes because we are created in the image of God.

When we take time to consider these realities, it exposes how pathetic are our pursuits to accumulate material possessions. And the irony is that we really don't possess these things; they begin to possess us.

People who are content with whatever they have materially are immensely attractive people to be around. They don't whine about what they don't have. The "simple things" in life amaze them. I love being around people like this. They are not striving to get ahead. They are at peace and seek to be faithful where God has placed them. Lest you make the mistake of thinking that this sounds like laziness, the proverbial lack of a good work ethic, it is not the case with the folks I know. These people work hard. They just aren't striving to keep up with the Joneses.

Contentment is a rare thing. In fact, one of my favorite books is titled *The Rare Jewel of Christian Contentment*. People who know how to appreciate the ordinary things of life have much to teach us. To remember how blessed beyond measure many of us are, consider this description about people living in the Middle Ages: "We, at the present day, can hardly understand the keenness with which a fur coat, a good fire on the hearth, a soft bed, a glass of wine, were formerly enjoyed." It is interesting that "the present day" mentioned above was 1924. How much more do the author's words apply to us today!

Much more memorable is what Bill Ball of Austin is famous for saying: "Rulers of two hundred years ago would have killed for a used Chevy Vega and access to petrochemicals." Maybe you are too young to remember this car of the seventies, but it is no longer an impressive automobile. In any case, Bill's brilliant point shows how easy it is to fall prey to discontent. We must have the latest gadgets and gizmos or we become terribly unhappy. Our discontent is definitely deepened if those around us have more stuff than we do.

There is much to be learned about contentment. Even the great apostle Paul had to learn about it. Make sure to soak in the implications of Philippians 4:13 in the "Discuss and Apply" section below.

Discuss and Apply

I have enjoyed the privilege of spending time with Walt Henrichsen, best-selling author and spiritual counselor to many men around the world. Walt likes to tell men that one of our problems is that we are greedy, but not greedy enough. He means that we tend to settle for material possessions and not be as interested in storing up heavenly treasures.

Meditate on Matthew 6:19–34. What keeps you from pursuing heavenly treasures? How can a friend help you grow in "godly greed"? Lest you think pursuing rewards is ungodly, keep in mind that Paul was motivated by heavenly rewards (see 2 Cor. 5:10; 2 Tim. 4:8). As Walt says, it is not greedy to breathe in as much air as you want for there is more than enough for everyone. In the same way, God has more than enough rewards for every faithful Christian. There is no lack whatsoever so we need not compete against one another. We all run unique races and we all can be amply rewarded (see 1 Cor. 9:24–27; 2 Tim. 4:8).

✦ ✦ ✦ ✦

One popular yet widely misinterpreted verse is extremely relevant to our topic. The verse is Philippians 4:13: "I can do all things through Christ who strengthens me." I have seen this on many weight-lifting belts, as if saying it enough times helped make you bench press more weight! Some realtors quote it to psych themselves into selling more homes. And certainly many more ways people misinterpret this verse could be added. So what is Paul saying? Look at the context. What are the "all things" that Paul is referring to? Major hint: it has to do with contentment.

+ + + +

If you want some sobering yet wise counsel in how to keep from being an "old fool," I highly recommend doing a study of Ecclesiastes 11:7–12:13. If you want to do further study of this important passage, I invite you to look at my commentary and the discussion questions included there. See Max Anders, ed., *Holman Old Testament Commentary: Ecclesiastes* by David George Moore (Nashville, TN: Broadman & Holman Publishers, 2003).

Notes

Years after observing the "buckets of beautiful golf balls" phenomenon, I read a related story about retirees collecting seashells. See John Piper, *Don't Waste Your Life* (Wheaton, IL: Crossway Books, 2003), 45–46. There are certainly a myriad of pointless diversions that can prevent us from being focused on the most important things in life.

In fact, one of my favorite books is titled, *The Rare Jewel of Christian Contentment*. An inexpensive paperback of this wonderful book by Jeremiah Burroughs can be purchased from The Banner of Truth Trust (Carlisle, PA).

To remember how blessed beyond measure many of us are . . . Quote is from J. Huizinga, *The Waning of the Middle Ages* (New York, NY: St. Martin's Press, 1984), 1.

Chapter 17

Walk among the Dead

My eighty-two-year-old dad likes to walk among the dead. Is he a freak? Hardly. He is blessed with dozens of men and women who consider him one of their closest friends. Is he morbid? Not at all. He is an optimist and has a good sense of humor. For many years now my dad regularly walks around the cemetery where one day he will be buried right next to where my mom is buried.

I cherish the special memories of being with my dad for his eightieth birthday bash. About twenty-five of his closest male friends came to "roast" him. My dad and I also made a trek over to the cemetery. Toward the end of our time there my dad pointed over to the new mausoleum. "Do you want to go take a tour?"

"Sure," I responded, "who wouldn't?"

We walked around this massive structure where row upon row of steel-encased drawers house the dead. There were also urns containing the remains of people from all walks of life. I was struck with seeing a picture of the deceased person nudged up against their respective urn. Pausing to observe the smiling faces in those pictures so full of life juxtaposed with urns full of ash was indeed sobering.

On our way out my dad started to sneeze. He quipped that maybe some of the dust from the urns was getting into his nose. His incessant sneezing caused me to think that a whole family had taken up residence in his sinuses. The man working the mausoleum that day assured us that "nothing gets out of those jars." This "gravedigger," for I'm not sure what to call someone who slides drawers in a mausoleum, asked us if we wanted to stay around a few minutes longer. A new "arrival" would be there shortly. We could watch the "festivities." "It's pretty interesting," our newfound friend added enthusiastically. We turned him down but left with some fresh insight about life and death.

Even though "death and taxes" come to all, we act as if only the latter do. I often ask people if they think much about their own impending death. Many don't or work really hard to not think about such things. Their response to my query is frequently associated with a nervous laugh.

Because we choose or, to be more accurate, are driven not to think about our own death, we tend to do idiotic things. We may not be quite like the woman who bought a $60,000 jigsaw puzzle and rationalized, "It's not the money I spend on puzzles that upset my ex-husband. It's the puzzles. I spent more time with them than I did him." However, our own actions may belie the fact that we care more about things than people. We need to remember some of Chuck Swindoll's most memorable words: "You don't see hearses pulling U-Hauls." As Job said, we come into this world "naked" and leave the very same way (see Job 1:21). Let that reality sink down deep in the recesses of your heart.

A little way north of our home is a large cemetery. It runs right alongside Interstate 35, a major thoroughfare in Texas. The juxtaposition of the highway with the cemetery is a metaphor for our times. We rush by on our merry way with no thought given to our ultimate destination. I try to imagine voices calling out to me as I drive by: "We see you, Dave Moore. Do you realize that our lot will soon be yours? Do you see us?"

Consider how differently death was treated earlier in our country's history. Lauren Winner writes:

> It is worth noting that through the nine-teenth century, Americans' idea of a good death was one in which you lingered; you grew ill and knew death was imminent and thus you had time to settle accounts, with your debtors and your family and also your Maker. It is only in this last century that Americans have wished to be caught unawares in our sleep, looking for

a death that is quick and painless and, also, a death for which we cannot prepare.

At other periods in our history people like the Puritans probably went too far with this "mortality motif." One eminent historian is quite critical. Referring to one strategy that Puritans used with respect to their children, this historian's distaste is apparent: "They [the children] were dragged screaming and twisting to the edge of an open grave and made to stare into the void and to reflect upon their own mortality." Another historian who has spent much of his life studying the Puritans weighs in with a little different perspective. When asked how the Puritans "affected him personally," his appreciation is clear:

> You can't read the number of Puritan sermons I've read and not confront the central question of those sermons: your mortality. The Puritans knew that this life doesn't go on forever, and that you need to live your life in the shadow of eternity. It's frightening to confront your mortality. Studying the Puritans made

me confront what we try so hard to avoid in
this society. But it confirmed in me the sense
that there needs to be an eternal hope.

I frequently ask Christians if they think death is
something they should be "at peace with." Most say
"yes." But this is not what Scripture says. We were
created to live forever in perfect fellowship with God.
Death is not our friend. Death is our final "enemy" (see
1 Cor. 15:26). Satan seeks to trap us in a net of fear
about death. Christ came to deliver us from bondage to
the fear of death (see Heb. 2:3–4). So we never reconcile
with our enemy death. He remains our foe, but he is an
enemy that no longer has power over us. Christ's bodily
resurrection is a promise that we who know Him will
receive a new body as well (see 1 Cor. 15:20–23). What
comfort! What crushing of fear!

I encourage you to walk among the dead. At the
very least, think more often about this impending reality. Maybe practice what some saints of old did as they
retired to bed at night. They would imagine that they

were lying down for the last time. Others like Jonathan Edwards talked about making the most of each day because you never know when it is your last one. You may also want to meditate on the verse that is at the top of my "lifelong to-do" list: "So teach us to number our days, that we may present to Thee a heart of wisdom" (Ps. 90:12).

Keeping death before us need not make us morose. John Adams is a good example for us to follow. His beloved daughter "Nabby" died of breast cancer. As David McCullough says, "The agony she endured in that day before anesthetics is unimaginable." Amazingly, even when Adams's own health was failing as he endured "severe pains in his back, rheumatism, no teeth, and loss of hearing," he could say, "I am not weary of life. I still enjoy it." In a letter to a close friend he wrote, "Griefs upon griefs! Disappointments upon disappointments. What then? This is a gay, merry world notwithstanding."

Discuss and Apply

No matter how much we jog or eat bran, we are not able to change the length of our life (see Job 14:5; Ps. 139:16). The *quality* of our life can certainly be positively affected by good habits of exercise, regular sleep, and eating right. How does this change your perspective on the time God has given you?

✦ ✦ ✦ ✦

Gary Thomas wrote an important article titled, "Wise Christians Clip Obituaries" (*Christianity Today*, 3 October 1994). Do you see any value in reading obituaries?

✦ ✦ ✦ ✦

Go to the note below on Jonathan Edwards. Read his seventy resolutions, especially the five that pertain to death. Consider drafting some resolutions of your own.

Notes

We may not quite be like the woman . . . Maryln Schwartz, "For Her, Life Is Just One Big Puzzle," *Dallas Morning News*, 13 October 1983.

Lauren Winner writes . . . *Mudhouse Sabbath* (Brewster, MA: Paraclete Press, 2003), 101.

They [the children] were dragged screaming and twisting . . . David Hackett Fischer, *Albion's Seed: Four British Folkways in America* (New York, NY: Oxford University Press, 1989), 113.

You can't read the number of Puritan sermons . . . Harry S. Stout, "The Puritans Behind the Myths," *Christian History* 41 (Carol Stream, IL: Christianity Today International, 41 [n.d.]): 43.

Maybe practice what some saints of old did as they retired to bed at night. One example is

William Law, *A Serious Call to a Devout and Holy Life* (Philadelphia, PA: The Westminster Press, 1955), 151. Here is an excerpt: "Represent to your imagination that your bed is your grave; that all things are ready for your interment; that you are to have no more to do with this world; and that it will be owing to God's great mercy if you ever see the light of the sun again or have another day to add to your works of piety. Then commit yourself to sleep as one that is to have no more opportunities of doing good, but is to awake among spirits that are separate from the body and waiting for the judgment of the last great day."

Others like Jonathan Edwards . . . Before he was twenty years old, Edwards wrote down seventy resolutions that he sought to keep. At least five of them (#5, 7, 9, 17, and 19) address the issue of living in light of one's impending death. You can google "The Resolutions of Jonathan Edwards" and read them online.

His beloved daughter "Nabby" died of breast cancer. David McCullough, *John Adams* (New York, NY: Simon & Schuster, 2001), 602.

Amazingly, even when Adam's own health was failing . . . David McCullough, *John Adams* (New York, NY: Simon & Schuster, 2001), 637 and 651.

Protecting Yourself

In 2001 I kept hearing about an extremely popular Christian book. Being somewhat of a contrarian, I determined not to read it. Predictably, people kept pressing me for my thoughts on the book that "everyone was reading." I was lovingly brought into submission and therefore commenced rather reluctantly to read it. My concerns eventually became a book review. As part of my review I came up with some principles for best determining the merits of popular Christian books. I leave you with these six principles along with some highly recommended books. I trust that they provide a spiritual protection of sorts.

1. Does the book convey (explicitly or implicitly) that it is *the key* to living the victorious Christian life?

2. Does the author present more of a formulaic approach to the Christian life rather than the need to grow in the "grace and knowledge of our Lord and Savior Jesus Christ" (see 2 Pet. 3:18)?

3. Does the book present a simplistic approach (read "cookie cutter") to the Christian growth or does it value the wide variety of ways that God sanctifies His people?

4. Does the author tend to universalize or make normative his own spiritual experiences?

5. Does the author ask the reader to trust his interpretation of his own spiritual experiences rather than backing those up with the word of God?

6. Most importantly, does the book focus on the person and work of Christ? In other words, is it a Christ-centered approach to the Christian life or is it a mechanical, moralistic, or behavioral approach?

Recommended Reading

Dan Doriani, *The Life of a God-Made Man* (Wheaton, IL: Crossway Books, 2001).

A solid biblical guide on the issues that men face.

_____

R. Kent Hughes, *Disciplines of a Godly Man* (Wheaton, IL: Crossway Books, 1991).

There are many good books on spiritual disciplines. This one hones in on their application to men.

_____

Dick Keyes, *True Heroism in a World of Celebrity Counterfeits* (Colorado Springs, CO, 1995).

The title gives you a good idea of the book's content. It is well written and contains many wonderful insights.

_____

Jeffrey E. Miller, *Hazards of Being a Man* (Grand Rapids, MI: Baker Book House, 2007).

A biblical and winsome treatment of twelve different "challenges all men face."

Brad Miner, *The Compleat Gentleman: The Modern Man's Guide to Chivalry* (Dallas, TX: Spence Publishing, 2004).

Beautifully written and provocative in the best sense of that word. Not your typical men's book. That is why it is so good.

Patrick Morley, *The Man in the Mirror* (Nashville, TN: Thomas Nelson Publishers, 1992).

The first men's book that I read and a good one. Short chapters on all the major issues of life.

Paul David Tripp, *Lost in the Middle: Midlife and the Grace of God* (Wapwallopen, PA: Shepherd Press, 2004).

Books addressing "midlife" crisis usually get goofy fast. This book is an exception. It is compassionate, realistic, and full of biblical wisdom.

Notes

In 2001 . . . I am grateful to John Armstrong, editor of *Viewpoint* magazine, for allowing me to excerpt a part of my review (David George Moore, "What Should We Think of the Prayer of Jabez?" July–August 2001).